Stories of

ROARING
F A I T H

COMPILED AND EDITED BY
DONNA SKELL
LISA BURKHARDT WORLEY
BELINDA MCBRIDE

Stories of Roaring Faith

Copyright © 2016 by Roaring Lambs Publishing

Published by:
Roaring Lambs Publishing
17110 Dallas Parkway, Suite 220
Dallas, TX 75248
Email: info@roaringlambs.org

Dedication

To God,
Thank You for the difference
You make in our lives.

To Garry Kinder,
Founder of Roaring Lambs Ministries,
Because of you, this book is possible.

To all the contributors of this book,
Thank you for sharing your personal testimonies
With the world.

To all the readers,
May your relationship
With our Lord Jesus Christ grow.

Introduction

About 30 years ago, I had the opportunity to attend a small class that taught me how to confidently and effectively share the Gospel against the backdrop of my life experiences. *It changed my life.* I learned the importance of sharing how God had proved Himself real to me.

Come and hear, all you who fear God; let me tell you what he has done for me. — *Psalm 66:16*

For the last several years, Roaring Lambs has been encouraging and equipping believers to effectively compose their testimony. Whether sharing one-on-one, speaking to a group, or just putting it in writing as a legacy for their future generations of family, it is beneficial.

We will tell the next generation the praiseworthy deeds of the Lord, his power, and the wonders he has done, so the next generation would know them, even the children yet to be born, and they in turn would tell their children. — *Psalm 78:4, 6*

Our testimony is our opportunity to let God use the circumstances He has allowed in our life for His glory. When you can take a difficult time and show how God used it for His good and yours, then you can give Him praise for that very hardship.

When he heard this, Jesus said, "This sickness will not end in death. No, it is for God's glory so that God's Son may be glorified through it." — John 11:4

Putting your faith story together will prepare you for many opportunities to share your faith. You are more likely to realize just how many there are daily.

But in your hearts revere Christ as Lord. Always be prepared to give an answer to everyone who asks you to give the reason for the hope that you have. But do this with gentleness and respect. — 1 Peter 3:15

The world needs to see how real Jesus is. Times are short. Your story matters; it is the living water that others need.

Then he said to his disciples, "The harvest is plentiful but the workers are few." — Matthew 9:37

Are you ready to be used by God and be richly blessed? Tell your story of what He has done for you.

Then I heard the voice of the Lord saying, "Whom shall I send and who will go for us?" And I said, "Here am I. Send me." — Isaiah 6:8

Donna Skell, Executive Director
Roaring Lambs Ministries

Acknowledgements

My sincere thanks are extended to Frank Ball for his gracious help turning this manuscript into a book. You are a kind, generous, God-loving man, and very appreciated by this ministry.

To Dan Thompson, our graphic designer from T-Bone Designs, many thanks for all of your work with Roaring Lambs, to give us such a great look. You are talented and have established our visual image. Thanks especially for a great cover for this book.

Thank you, Shannon Johnson, for your work editing the testimonies. I know you were blessed by reading them, but we are blessed by all your spelling, punctuation, and grammar corrections.

For Doug Kingsriter, we are grateful for your encouragement of our work to help Christians effectively and confidently share their amazing stories of God's love, grace, power, healing, and forgiveness.

To my co-compilers and editors, Belinda McBride and Lisa Burkhardt Worley, without the two of you, this book would have never been completed. Thank you for your endless hours of reading and re-reading the stories. Thank you for your attention to the small details.

Thank you, again, to all who contributed their personal testimonies. This book is not about you, but is all about our great and awesome God we serve.

The Power of
Story Transformation

Wherever there's a fight, a struggle, or contention in our lives, there is a story. Why? Without conflict, there is no story. When we ultimately prevail over conflict, we experience relief and great joy. The Apostle Paul summed his life up this way— "I have fought the good fight, I have finished the race, I have kept the faith." Throughout his trials, Paul discovered the secret of experiencing joy despite his circumstances; his testimony of encouragement for us.

There's an important distinction, however, between stories and testimonies. Stories are the byproduct of conflict—personal testimonies are the byproduct of God's intervention in adversarial circumstances, in the stories of our lives. Stories of challenge and difficulty are literally testimonies waiting to happen.

Without Jesus in our lives, our stories of conflict are bleak. But when the Lord comes into our circumstances, a metamorphosis takes place—what was once our story becomes our testimony. Revelation 19:10 indicates that when we give our testimony, we open the atmosphere for our miracle to be repeated. Our testimony carries with it the power of change. When we speak out of our experience with God, we are not just giving information, but are sharing God's power of transformation, a transformation that affects others.

The Israelites' story was their walking away from Egypt after 400 years of bondage to arrive at the Red Sea, but they were still in fear. The transformation of their story began to unfold when the Angel of the Lord, who had been in front of Israel from their departure, moved behind them as a cloud that brought darkness to the oppressor and light to the

Israelites, enabling their walk across the now-parted Red Sea. On the other side of the Red Sea, when they realized their captor had been eliminated and they were now in complete freedom, they sang their testimony of what God had done.

As 2 Corinthians 5:17 says, "This means that anyone who belongs to Christ has become a new person. The old life is gone; a new life has begun!" You might be a believer, but has the "new" begun in your life circumstances?

When it does, you will not be able to contain it.

Just as we receive Christ into our lives and are transformed by His grace, so it is when Jesus steps into our story of despair. He reconstitutes the story components, and then creates an unimaginable outcome to form a testimony of power that can transform others who are living in what used to be your circumstance.

Our greatest challenge? What we want to conceal, God wants to reveal. Do not deny the power of your testimony that God intended to use in transforming the lives of others! Tell the miracle—that Jesus transformed what was once a story of reproach into a testimony of freedom and deliverance.

Be bold. Spread the fire by articulating the power that's released when Kingdom saints herald the miraculous work God has done in their lives. – Doug Kingsriter

Doug Kingsriter is an author, speaker, and has been a leader in development for organizations like Mothers Against Drunk Driving (MADD), the Lance Armstrong Foundation and the Be the Match Foundation. Doug, who now lives in the Dallas/Fort Worth Metroplex, is also a former professional football player for the Minnesota Vikings.

Table of Contents

Monopoly of the Heart
by David Souther

When I was seven years old, I received one of my favorite birthday gifts of all time. It was a Monopoly Game. It wasn't just any Monopoly game; it was the *Deluxe* edition with a faux leather case, built-in compartments to hold the money and pieces, gold plated tokens, and real wooden houses. Playing the normal edition at someone else's house felt like "second-class" Monopoly.

The object of the game is simple: make money to buy stuff. When you get enough stuff, you can then make more money and buy more stuff to use with your original stuff. Then you use all of your stuff to get more money to get more stuff. Do you see a pattern here? The person with the most money and stuff at the end wins.

Now there is nothing wrong with this game per se. However, we get into trouble when we confuse the Monopoly world with the *real* world. We know the world of Monopoly isn't real. You would be foolish or deluded to try to pay your bills with Monopoly money. However, if we are not careful, the goal of Monopoly, to get more and more stuff, can become our goal in life.

That was me. My goal in life was to get more money to buy more stuff. But it wasn't just about the money and stuff, it is what the money and stuff gave me: comfort, ease, pleasure, peace, and security. I felt if I had enough stuff, I would be content. If I could just make this next purchase of a stereo, computer, car, whatever, I would be happy.

It was as though I felt a hole in my heart and was trying to fill it with possessions. So I built my life around money and stuff, going from deposit to deposit, purchase to purchase. Stuff became a type of drug for me. That uneasy feeling in my being, "Hey, let's go buy something." Have you ever felt that sense of emptiness? "I have the cure. Let's plan a new major purchase." I found temporary happiness in researching the purchase, looking at the options, making the purchase, then repeating the cycle.

The bottom line was I didn't own possessions; possessions owned me. I didn't control my money; it controlled me.

This is more common than you think. Some men may agree, "Yes it is. Just look at my wife and her shopping habits!" However, men can fall into this trap too. We may not buy as much stuff as some women, but the stuff we buy costs a whole lot more. It is also an issue that can affect every income level and every tax bracket, not just the upper "1 percent" of people who have the most money. The reason is that it is not a matter of the size of your bank account, but the condition of your heart.

Slowly I began to realize two things. First, no matter how much money or stuff I had, it was never enough. I would make a purchase, but the emptiness soon returned. For example, I decided it was time for me to get a new vehicle. The old one was just fine, but I thought it would be awesome to get a new one. The search for just the right one consumed me. I remember the day I bought the vehicle, a Jeep Grand Cherokee, and getting into the car to drive it off the lot. There it was, the smell of a brand new car! I was overjoyed, at least for a few weeks. Then the wax job started to dull, the tires began to wear, and the inside was not as clean and fresh as before. The new car smell gradually dissipated. Before I knew it, I was driving a used car again. More than that, the emptiness and hunger I felt in my heart to drive me to that purchase returned.

You see, I was looking for stuff to do what it was incapable of doing, providing lasting joy and satisfaction. It was like trying to drink seawater to satisfy a physical thirst. It gives temporary relief, but then you are worse off than you were before, even more thirsty because of the salt content. I was striving for contentment, trying to counteract the empty feelings I had deep down; but no matter how much I bought or had, it was never enough. It just made me thirsty for more.

The second thing I realized is that life mirrors Monopoly in at least one respect. At the end of the game, what happens? All the money and stuff you worked so hard to accumulate goes back in the box. You don't take it with you. You may have earned a ton of money, own all the property, and have all the stuff, but when the game is over, it is over. The stuff goes back in the box. It is the same in life.

At the end you keep nothing.

This really hit home for me when I was having some remodeling done on my house. The carpet installer was there and I began to ask him about himself. I'll never forget what he said, "Laying carpet doesn't pay all that much, but I enjoy it. Besides, my goal is not to be the richest man in the graveyard."

The second sentence stunned me. You see, my goal up to that point had been to make as much money as possible. I justified it by telling myself, "I'll make as much money as I can, then give a lot away to the church. I'll do many good things with it." There is nothing wrong with that motive, but when it becomes your main passion and priority in life, you have a problem. And I had a problem big-time because the main reason I wanted money was because of the stuff it bought and the comfort, ease, and privilege it provided.

After hearing what the man said, I began to think, "What am I living for? Is this the main purpose of life, to accumulate stuff just to have it rot in a landfill 100 years from now?" I knew deep down that it wasn't, but my actions and behavior indicated otherwise.

I also started thinking about what is going to last. And I began to consider Jesus Christ. I had gone to church my entire life and experienced good as well as bad. But I began to focus on Christ Himself. You may say, "Jesus lived 2000 years ago; what does He have to do with this?" That is a valid question, but here are three key facts, relevant to what I was experiencing. First, Jesus had very little in terms of earthly possessions, but was one of the most significant people in history. Second, although he was not rich, He was content, a contentment I longed for. Lastly, He was never preoccupied by possessions, but committed Himself to people, loving and serving them.

I saw great power in that. Now here is someone worth listening to.

I also considered some of the statements Jesus made that are recorded in the Bible, especially this one: "Let anyone who is thirsty come to me and drink" (John 7:37). He is not talking about physical thirst, but that deep down thirst of the soul for contentment, peace, and significance, things I was searching for.

I was convinced Jesus is the one who could satisfy the longings of my heart. The Bible refers to Jesus when it says, "All things were made through Him, and without Him nothing was made that was made" (John 1:3 ESV). Who knows better how to fulfill the longings and desires of the heart than the One who made our hearts in the first place?

It also dawned on me I was seeking to meet the longings of my heart through money and stuff instead of Him. It was like I was trying to fill my physical hunger with donuts rather than a nutritious meal. I was so full of junk, the fleeting satisfaction that money and possessions bring, that I had left

4

no room for God. However, I was so used to this way of living, I felt trapped by it.

I was certain that only Jesus had the power to deliver me from my obsession and dependence on stuff, the stuff I so wanted to fill the emptiness I felt in my heart. Only He had the power to deliver me because Jesus is not only a man, He is God Almighty. He is the Creator and Sustainer of all things. Nothing is too difficult for Him, not even my selfish addiction to stuff!

After years of living for "stuff," I turned to Jesus to satisfy the hunger in my heart and restlessness in my spirit and to give me true peace and contentment. I also turned to Him to rescue me from my obsession with money and stuff. And He did. And I continue to find my satisfaction in Him each day, not based on how much money or stuff I have, but in the satisfaction of knowing and following Him.

Here are three things I have also come to know. First, because of Jesus, God loves me regardless of how much money or stuff I have. Secondly, I have found true contentment in God. He has supplied the joy, security, and significance I craved. I no longer am enslaved to stuff. Jesus has freed me from that bondage. He has allowed me to stop focusing on money and possessions to satisfy. Third, when it is all said and done, my relationship with God is the only thing that matters, because it is the only thing I am taking with me when this life is over. Everything else is going back in the box.

David Souther is the President of EvanTell, a ministry serving the church with evangelism outreach and training. David's calling and passion is that more people hear the gospel in more places every day. A native Tennessean, he is married to Donna. They have three daughters and live in Dallas, Texas.

Thoughts to Ponder
from Monopoly of the Heart

1. Money and possessions will never fill the void in your heart.

2. True success is measured by what you have left after you subtract everything money can buy.

3. How you use your resources is a direct reflection on what is in your heart.

What gets between you and God?

But remember the Lord your God,
for it is he who gives you the ability
to produce wealth. — Deuteronomy 8:18

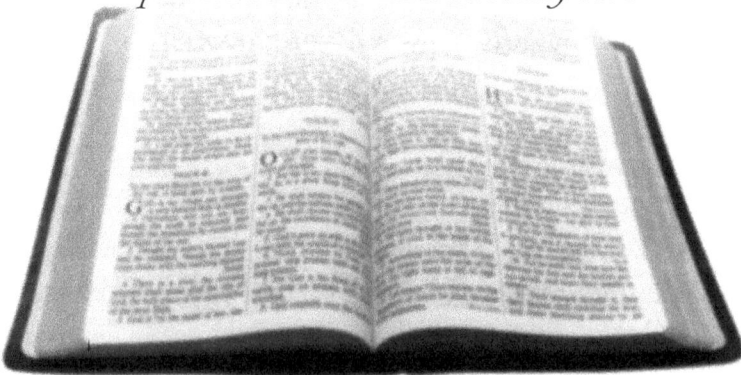

Hostage
by Kathleen Watson

It was once a magnificent chair, carved by a master's hand, exquisite, intricate, with a great hope and a purpose. And in the beginning, it was lovely. As life went on, however, it became unappreciated, exposed to the elements, worn, and even abused. Its original beauty and any perceived value appeared to be destroyed.

Since my earliest memories I felt like this chair: insignificant, ugly, stupid, unwanted, and unloved. Can anyone relate? Maybe that is why as a very young girl, I chose to go into the field of interior design. It was a profession of unlimited potential, where the unlovely did not stay that way. It was escaping what something was, to become something totally different, to be the contrast of where you started: something better, desirable, appreciated, and even loved.

My story illustrates a journey that in some ways, we all take. Where, like this chair, our promising beginning encounters many harsh, unkind years that seem to dash our hopes. Where also, like the many homes I have remodeled, transformation is possible.

My mother grew up in a dysfunctional, abusive home. She had very low self-confidence and always seemed beaten down. She received all of her worth and value from my Dad as he sparingly dispersed it. When I was born, she saw me as competition for my dad's affections and felt threatened. Years later when my daughter, her first grandchild, was born, she admitted this to me in tears, saying that is why she was never able to love me like my brothers and sisters. To me, she was distant and uninvolved. I assumed it was me; I was not good enough, not worthy to be loved.

My father was a workaholic and gone most of the time. When he was home, he was critical and a perfectionist. My parents fought often. Our home was not a happy place. Once in a blue moon, however, something I would do pleased him, and then he would praise me, and I was his princess. The affirmations were few and far between, but it was all that I ever got from anyone, and it was precious! He was the one person whom I felt loved me at all.

In first grade at a small school, I received A's, B's, and one C. My father was extremely disappointed, and against the school's recommendation he held me back to repeat first grade. At that point, I also believed I was stupid.

There was a bully from my original first grade class who decided his life goal was to make me miserable. He made it known to all the new, shy, incoming first graders that I was a loser and a flunky, and if anyone became my friend, they would regret it.

So my new classmates avoided me like a plague, and for the seven years I was in that school, I ate lunch alone and sat by myself on the playground.

At home, life was not much better. My perfect, intelligent, athletic, older brother, whom my parents adored, also constantly called me names, made fun of me, and was continually cruel. With no correction or intervention from my parents, their silence seemed to be their endorsement. So, that was my identity. I *was* stupid, ugly, and a loser. I felt alone and unwanted.

Have you ever felt that way?

Ironically, my family was religious in a dry, legalistic sort of way. When I was ten, my father became ill, and this empty religion no longer satisfied; so they began to search for more. That's when a neighbor invited my parents to an informal Bible study he was having in his home. They learned that the Jesus they had read about their whole lives was more than a historical figure from a book. He is today a living, active, fully alive Savior, who is not only interested in our individual lives, but desires to know us on a personal level. Grasping that changed everything!

The Bible they memorized came alive as the Holy Spirit filled the words. Their lives took on a third dimension as they began to have an intimate relationship with Jesus Christ. Both my dad and mom gave Jesus lordship of their lives, and our home became an entirely different place.

My dad became encouraging and kind, and my mom started to smile and sing around the house. I, too, gave my heart to the Lord and was filled with a hope and a joy I had never known. I still had no one to sit with at school, but I was no longer alone, for Christ was my new best friend.

Over the next year, although my father's condition worsened, we were full of hope, believing God would heal him. It was the happiest year of my childhood. Then at the age of thirteen, everything changed when my Dad died. All hope seemed to evaporate. Now I also felt abandoned.

My mom found herself alone without any extended family, a widow with four young children, without a job, deeply in debt, grief stricken, confused, and overwhelmed. She found a secretarial job, earning minimum wage, came home every night, went directly to her bedroom, and cried herself to sleep.

My brothers, sister, and me, ages six to fourteen, went to work doing whatever odd jobs we could find to help make enough money, so we wouldn't lose our house. We mowed lawns, took newspaper routes, babysat, de-tasseled corn, you name it. There was never any milk or fruit in the fridge and often no heat in the cold Illinois winters. Mom no longer seemed to function, but appeared more like the "walking dead." We did not eat a family meal together or celebrate a holiday or birthday again. I was numb and in survival mode.

At the age of sixteen, I decided there were three possible explanations as to why my life was so awful:

#1- God is mean and cruel,

#2- God is uninvolved and does not care,

or #3- God did not exist at all!

These three options left me with the same conclusion, that I would no longer be a "Christian."

That is when I met a boy named Steve, who I worked with at a shoe store in the mall. He was twenty-three and a graduate student at the local university. I remember at sixteen thinking, *He is so old.* He was tall, 6'4", handsome, clean cut, and always kind and polite. He never flirted in any way or asked me out, so I thought of him as sort of a big brother and really my only friend. We would spend hours talking to each other when the store was slow.

One day, Steve invited me to his apartment for a Super Bowl party. When I showed up with my cheese tray, no one else was there. I asked where everyone else was, and he said they would be there any minute. Then Steve asked if he could show me something "really quick" and motioned for me to follow him. I did, without a second thought.

At the end of the hall, before I could realize what was happening, he pulled me into a dark room, slammed the door, and locked a series of deadbolts. The light bulbs were removed, and the window was boarded over; weapons, rope, and duct tape lay on the dresser. He then proceeded to tell me he knew I was a loner and had no friends, that my mom was basically non-existent, and that no one would miss me for days.

He said we were a couple stories up, and there was no way to escape. I could scream all I wanted, but all the other tenants were gone for Christmas break and no one would hear me. Then he flatly told me he planned to kill me, but not quite yet.

He threw me down on an old mattress that was on the floor; then sometime later when he was done, he left the room. This repeated itself over and over. The mild mannered Dr. Jekyll had become Mr. Hyde, someone I had never seen before, evil and full of rage and hate. I was a virgin, saving myself for Mr. Right; I guessed now we would never meet.

I remember thinking how odd it was I did not have any tears. I suppose they had all been used up years earlier. At the time, I believed I deserved it. I wondered how I ever could have thought that there was even a slight possibility to have a "happily ever after." As I lay there, full of fear and pain, I wondered if I should cry out to God for help. *No, I thought, if there actually is a God, he would not help me; besides, if there is a God, I burned that bridge.*

My life was worthless, not worthy of saving anyway, right? Then I thought of my dad. The thought that he was sitting in heaven, able to see me like this, broke my heart. I decided to escape. I whispered a silent cry to God for help and waited for an opportunity. Thinking I was resigned to my fate, Steve let his guard down. He walked out the door to get something and left it open. That was my opportunity!

Without a stitch of clothes on, I ran stark naked out the bedroom door. My purse was still on the table with my keys lying beside. I grabbed them and was barely out the front door, and Steve was already at my heels. I dove down three flights of stairs, and jumped into my clunker, which thankfully I never locked. He leaped onto the car yelling, slamming his fists on the windshield. My heart was pounding through my chest! Then, as the car flew around the corner, he was flung from the car. I escaped!

God heard my cry for help, and delivered me; but even still, it did not soften my heart of stone. I quickly chalked it up to luck and remained distant from God, behind the tall walls I erected around my heart.

I never told a soul what happened; and in fact I kept it boarded up in a secret place in my heart for many, many years. That night of my escape, I pulled myself up by my own bootstraps, and decided to pretend like it never happened. However, we all know that never really works.

A few months later I met another boy, Brad. He too was tall, athletic, handsome, and a seeming "prince charming." We started dating. He treated me like I was valuable and told me I was smart and beautiful. Oh no! I feared I was falling in love. How could I not?

But I was so afraid; I *just* knew this was too good to be true, and I would end up hurt again. Either Brad would snap and turn evil, or he would wake up and realize I was a disappointment and leave. Every day I held my breath, hoping today was not that day. But the days turned into weeks, and the months into years, and to my surprise he remained true and devoted. After three years of dating, to my astonishment, we were married.

Wow! I found myself looking at my life in utter amazement. I had a happy marriage with an adoring amazing husband, a beautiful condo on the lake, my dream job as an interior designer on Chicago's prestigious North Shore, and plenty of money. It was more than I had ever even dared to hope for. It truly was the perfect life. Right?

So why was I not happy? Why did everything seem empty, shallow, and gray? In the stillness of the night, night after night, as these questions rolled through my head, I kept hearing a still soft voice say,

"You know what is missing, it is Me. Return to Me."

Shivers rolled down my spine, and I replied to the darkness,

"No. I cried out to God to save my dad, and God didn't."

The voice said, "But I saved you."

And I yelled in reply, "No, I saved myself. All the hardship I faced was your fault! If you are real, you let me down."

Then I would remind myself how great my life was, tell myself this 'gray emptiness' was crazy. Of course I was happy. I was not missing anything or anyone.

Fortunately, God is a gentleman, and not pushy; but He is also not easily dissuaded. He would not give up. After being married for almost two years, one day at work I came across the poem *Footprints*. It was about a man who had a dream that he and the Lord were walking together on the beach. They were viewing scenes from the man's life. The man realized that whenever he went through a very difficult time, there was only one set of footprints. He asked the Lord, "Why did you abandon me when I needed you most?" The Lord replied, "I never left you my child; those single footprints were mine. That is when I was carrying you!"

As I read the poem, it was as though the Lord himself was speaking to me. Those words went deep into my heart. His firm, strong voice, washed over me. "I never left you, Kathleen. I was holding you in my arms. It is because I was there with you, that you are here and have survived! I am the reason your life today is blessed. You can trust me. Come back to me, and let me love you."

The three reasons I thought I had to invalidate my faith were instantly eliminated.

#1- God is not unkind or unloving. John 3:16 says God loved the world so much that He gave his only Son for us. It is our choice to turn to Him or away from Him. To thank Him for the good, or blame Him for the bad. Satan is more than happy to help us come up with accusations against God and justifications for our bad decisions. God never stopped loving me! He still loves me, and every one of you as well, more than we could ever comprehend.

#2- God never abandoned me. Deuteronomy 31:6 says, "For it is the Lord your God who goes with you; He will never leave you nor forsake you." They say, "Hind sight is 20/20." That's the truth. Now, in retrospect, His continual presence is apparent. He was, and is always there, is involved every minute, and cares beyond what I could ever comprehend.

#3- God is not only real, He is alive! Revelation 1:18 says He is alive "forever and ever." At that moment, I knew all of this in my heart beyond a shadow of a doubt, and He continually reveals Himself to me.

There at my desk, I broke down, sobbed, and rededicated myself to God. Everything God said that day was true: I was alive in this body, yes, but in my spirit as well, and for all of eternity. I was loved perfectly by the Lord himself, who would never abandon or disappoint me. I was blessed beyond measure with treasure that would not rot or rust, that of joy, peace, hope, and contentment. Now I truly had the wonderful life, the life I never before even allowed myself to dream of. It all was a product of God's loving kindness and grace.

I felt I deserved hardship, so it did not draw me to Christ. Rather, it was the unmerited favor that brought me to my knees. The goodness of God led me to repentance.

The heavy cloud was lifted off of my life, and everything was bright, beautiful, three-dimensional, and technicolor. There was once again joy deep within my soul. The same joy that I knew as a ten-year-old girl, that same joy that today characterizes my life, to all who know me.

That was twenty-five years ago. My life has not been perfect; it has had its heartbreaks and struggles, its ups and downs like everyone else's. However, since that time, I have not spent one day feeling worthless, unloved, hopeless or

14

alone. I say this not because of any person in my life, but because of the Holy Spirit who lives inside of me.

We have all been born into a world full of hardship, sickness, and death. Being a follower of Christ does not negate this, but it gives us the resources and ability to not just survive, but thrive in the midst of it. Life on our own, apart from God, no matter how beautiful or successful, is unfulfilling, empty and vain. I know this first hand. But we have the choice to invite in the Creator of the universe, to remedy that hopelessness, and make our lives bright and beautiful. He restores the worn out, old chair.

At one time, my life was like the discarded chair, ready for the dumpster. Its beauty and perceived value appeared to be destroyed. But then the King claimed it, and in His hands it was boldly redeemed from imminent destruction and delicately restored. All the years of damage, exposure, neglect, and abuse melted away, to reveal its original beauty. Now, it is as magnificent as the day it was created and even more precious because of the high value given by its owner.

Kathleen Watson's passion is to see believers realize and embrace their true identity in Christ; finding freedom from the past, and joy in their present spiritual walk. She is a speaker with Stonecroft Ministries, travels internationally, speaking with Global Advance, and is an ardent Bible study teacher.

Thoughts to Ponder
from The Hostage

1. God may be invisible, but He is always present.

2. God will provide a way out of trouble.

3. God is able to mend tattered lives.

What has God rescued you from?

He rescued me from my powerful enemy,
from my foes, who were too strong for me.
— Psalm 18:17

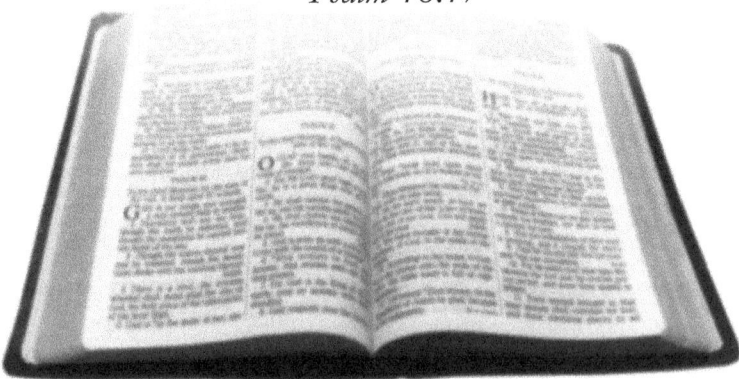

Cancer Doesn't Scare Me
by Aubrey McNutt

I have cancer.

It has been diagnosed as Stage-4 Adenocarcinoma and is considered terminal. It is my desire that you understand I have great confidence and peace, despite the prognosis. Having a terminal disease crystallizes in my mind that my salvation is secure. To be able to rejoice in suffering makes more sense to me than ever.

Jesus Christ and the apostle Paul give two great examples of the attitude I want to take as I face the reality of death and eternity. To tell you the truth, I am excited about what I consider the greatest day in the life of a Christian, the very last day, the last breath, the last heartbeat.

In Matthew 26:39, Jesus prayed in the Garden of Gethsemane to His Father, "My Father, if it is possible, may this cup be taken from me. Yet not as I will, but as you will." Lord, help me to have that kind of submission!

And in 2 Corinthians 12:7–10, Paul talks about the "thorn in the flesh" as he pleads with God three times to remove it from him. The Lord responds, "My grace is sufficient for you, for my power is made perfect in weakness" (2 Corinthians 12:9). Paul later says that's why he delights in weaknesses, in insults, in hardships, in persecutions, and in difficulties. "For when I am weak, then I am strong" (2 Corinthians 12:10). Cancer makes me weak, but I am stronger than I have ever been before because of God's grace.

There are many nights when I can't sleep, often because of the pain, often because of the terrible chemicals that are rushing through my veins; but the most predominate sensation that always overwhelms me is feeling the very presence of Jesus by my side. It is as if I can reach out in the darkness and touch Him. He knows my pain, and I have this awesome feeling of peace that truly surpasses all understanding.

My cancer is an intestinal cancer that has spread to many places throughout my body. I've undergone two major surgeries, 66 radiation treatments, and 49 chemotherapy treatments. This cancer was discovered when doctors found a large tumor in my bladder in the fall of 2008.

In January of 2009, a minor surgery removed the tumor; but three years later, it was discovered that the cancer had returned and spread. So, my first major surgery in 2012 removed the bladder, about half of my large intestines, my prostate, and several lymph glands. The doctor explained to us that Stage 4 cancer means remission is not likely, and that the chances of survival are slim past five years of diagnosis.

My diagnosis of cancer has been an amazing blessing because it has helped me understand, like never before, the ultimate purpose of why God created me. It made me realize that every part of my brief life on earth is useless without Jesus Christ.

How I live this life determines where I'll spend eternity. My most important duty is to glorify God, obey His commands, and share the Gospel of Jesus Christ with all the abilities God has given me.

To maintain my commitment to Christ, I began reading my Bible more consistently.

My prayer life improved.

I became hungry for finding Christian literature to enhance my spiritual knowledge.

And Christian music, which has always been important to me, became a huge factor in helping me to remain more focused, committed, and inspired during my battle with cancer. I have many awesome songs saved on my iTunes, and so, at any moment, when I need to stop and refocus, I can play my favorites and be lifted up to where I need to be.

One song, by a famous gospel group, has inspired me more than any song I can think of. It has reminded me to walk with joy because my debts are paid, and that I am a child of God, so I should not be afraid. This particular song gives me chills of inspiration every time I hear it. It expresses the very reasons why I can have peace, joy, and confidence, even in the midst of a major trial. If a person's testimony could match the words of this song, just try to imagine how the Kingdom of God would grow!

Many people have complimented and thanked me for my positive attitude despite terminal cancer, but I easily see the real credit and praise goes directly to God. He has given me the tools to maintain my focus.

Many times people have told me they wish they had as much faith as I have. However, that is not the most important factor. After all, faith the size of a mustard seed can move a mountain. Belief in the Gospel of Jesus Christ and trust in God's amazing grace are, by far, more important and powerful than anything we can do to experience His peace.

So, I have assessed some of the ways I handle cancer and have contemplated, "Why?" "Why did I feel this way?" "Why do I have a flood of peace that overwhelms me?" It did not just suddenly happen.

As I thought about it, I realized my strength and confidence go way back.

Blessed to be raised in a Christian home, my parents taught me from day one there is a God who created everything. He loves us unconditionally. The Trinity is made up of God, Jesus, and the Holy Spirit.

When you reach the "age of accountability," you realize you have a need. The "age of accountability" is when you actually come to a conviction that you are in sin and that you need redemption. It usually comes around four, six, or eight years of age, but it can come years or decades later. For some it may be 40, 60, or 80 years of age.

I was probably eight or nine years old when evil temptations started getting my attention. Accountability came into focus big time. Two particular incidents convicted me of the evil in my heart.

I was the youngest of eight children, with five of us living at home at the same time. We lived in a small two-bedroom house. My dad and mom had one bedroom and three sisters had the other bedroom. That left the cold back porch for my brother, who was six-and-a-half years older, and myself. We slept under a lot of blankets in the wintertime.

For ten years, we lived on the outskirts of town in the city of Shawnee, Oklahoma, about 35 miles due east of Oklahoma City. It was in elementary school that things began to happen and revealed to me the devil was real, and that I had tendencies to give in to his temptations.

One of my first encounters with Satan's ways was walking to and from the city municipal swimming pool, about ten blocks from home. Sometimes I walked with my sisters, and sometimes I walked by myself. About halfway between home and the swimming pool was a drug store. Inside that drug store were magazine racks with pornographic literature that I would thumb through. I eventually realized the evil nature of what I was allowing myself to indulge in, and that it was a bad choice. It scared me deeply to think I was giving in to the devil. I realized Satan was sneaking into my heart, so I intentionally avoided this evil temptation.

Meanwhile, at the swimming pool I became friends with a tall, dark, and handsome man, with whom I was very impressed. He treated me nice. He bought me candy, and I even invited him to our home a time or two to have dinner with our family. He was kind and respectful to my parents and siblings. But, one day after swimming, he took me into the county courthouse, located near the swimming pool, and led me into a restroom on the very same floor as the sheriff's office. That is where he sexually molested me. I was devastated, but never ever told anyone about what had happened until just recently, 58 years later! All I could think about was how evil I was, when in reality, this man was a predator.

Reaching my age of accountability convicted me of my sinful nature.

I finally reached a certain level of maturity to know I desperately needed Jesus in my life. Fortunately, my parents gave us a Christian home where we always attended church every time the doors were opened. From day one, I was taught about Jesus, and when the time was right, I realized I had a way out of the evil clutches of the devil.

I knew that Jesus was the Son of God.

I knew my faith in Him was real.

I knew Jesus Christ commanded me to publicly confess my sins and to be baptized for the remission of my sins.

My faith, belief, confession, and baptism at eleven years of age were necessary to overcome my sinful nature.

As I think about the events in my life since my baptism into Christ, I easily see that the common thread of my life has always been the wise, but very subtle promptings of the Holy Spirit and knowing that Jesus was always by my side. So many events that turned out right for me were things I did not even realize at the time. They were the result of the Spirit's protection. Wow! I would not have survived many situations had it not been for the Spirit of God gently nudging me into the right direction.

I want to give you a few examples.

When I went off to college, I did not stop attending church like many of my fellow classmates. That was the guidance of the Holy Spirit!

Then came two years in the United States Marine Corps. After boot camp in San Diego, California, I found a Christian family that picked me up for every church service. None of my Marine buddies would go with me. But I could not stop going to church. That was the Holy Spirit!

Speaking of being in the Marines, my MOS (military occupation) was Field Radio Operator. After boot camp, I went back to San Diego for radio school. On the first day of school, we were notified that every one of our class of about 35 had orders already written up to be deployed to Vietnam. This was 1969 when the war was raging strong. You must understand that a Field Radio Operator's average life expectancy in Vietnam was short. They were prime targets for snipers in any kind of combat operation. But after graduation from radio school, only one of the class of 35 had their orders cancelled, and that one was me. Again, that happened because of the protection of the Holy Spirit and the fervent prayers of a righteous momma.

At age 28, my first marriage failed, but I still attended church. That was the Holy Spirit!

At 31 years of age, I was led to Dallas, Texas in 1979. I bet you think getting out of Oklahoma was an act of the Holy Spirit. Yes, it was. Soon after I got to Dallas, my sister JoAnne and I joined an awesome church that has been my church home ever since.

Within two months, I met the love of my life, Kathy. After Kathy and I met at a large singles function on March 31, 1979, we started dating and it quickly escalated into serious affections for each other, but it scared Kathy to death. She had also gone through a terrible divorce. With a six-year-old and a two-year-old, she could not stand the thought of giving her heart to another man. And so, after six months, she broke off our relationship.

I was devastated, but I remembered how my mom taught me to pray. So I started praying. I guess Kathy didn't think to pray for me to just go away. I prayed for the Lord to please change Kathy's heart, so my prayers were answered! We have been married for 36 years now, and the Lord has blessed us in unbelievable ways. Many people look at Kathy and me and they are confounded that I did so well to "marry up" like I did. I just say I had high expectations, and she didn't. She did have one prenuptial agreement that she wanted me to agree to. She made me promise that I would never move her to Oklahoma. Of course, I accepted that stipulation. I figured I had a better chance of succeeding in Texas, because when I moved to Texas from Oklahoma, I improved the IQ of both states!

For all of us, there are many problems that relentlessly consume our lives. There needs to be and there always is a solution.

My early awareness of my sinful nature and my decision to do something about it by choosing to believe in Jesus Christ was my wisest choice. I was not fully aware of the magnitude of my confession and commitment, but at eleven years of age, I knew I was on the right track.

I am fearless in this journey with cancer, because I clearly feel the amazing love God pours out on me. He holds me in the palm of His hand. I constantly feel the presence of Jesus, intimately by my side. A trivial matter such as terminal cancer is no match for the love of God. So, since I comprehend that God loves me, and that I love Him, I am free. I am content. I am at peace, and I cannot wait to go home.

I am not a prisoner of cancer.

I am not a prisoner to sin.

And in the Holy Spirit, the common thread that has woven my life together, He guides me, and the trust and peace I have in Christ's perfect sacrifice always keeps me on the right track. All of my negative challenges never get the best of me. Instead, they solidify my commitment to God.

Over the last seven years, I have constantly researched many good Christian books that could help me understand more clearly the meaning of the deep truths of the Bible and to grasp this phenomenal blessing of peace. Because of my cancer, and because of the valuable insights I have gained from godly Bible scholars, my diligent study of the Scriptures has been more consistent and vibrant.

One of my favorite verses in the Bible is Psalm 139:16. It says, "All the days ordained for me were written in your book before one of them came to be."

I am invincible until my last day comes, and God knew it before the foundations of the world were formed.

My peace and joy is certain and it is in large part because of my journey with cancer. There is no terminal illness or no devil that can take that from me.

Because of my absolute assurance of my salvation, I have nothing to worry about, and my prayer request is that Jesus Christ will be glorified through me in the greatest way possible. May my "thorn in the flesh," cancer, not be removed if it is the best way for me to glorify God.

I am his child and I am not alone. I am not afraid.

I am thankful for this reality of a terminal disease of cancer. It is truly a wonderful blessing to me. The fact that the number of my days are rapidly dwindling makes everything I do more focused on what I can do to prepare myself for eternity and to influence others to become more keenly aware that the number of their days are just as tenuous as mine. None of us is promised tomorrow; in fact, I do not know a perfectly healthy person that can guarantee they will outlive me.

Therefore, I share my testimony with you, hoping and praying that something I have written will encourage you. May it help you to be ready for this inevitable event called death, which is probably much closer than you think.

What are your prospects for eternity?

Seriously ponder what you are doing that will determine your eternal destination.

The proper decision is clear and absolute. It is a dedicated allegiance to the King of kings and the Lord of lords!

If you have not made that decision and commitment, the time is now, before it is too late.

Aubrey McNutt, a retired carpenter, is active in his church and spends his time helping others. He was born and raised in Shawnee, Oklahoma, but moved to Dallas in 1979. He is married to his beautiful wife, Kathy, and has three children, twelve grandchildren, and four great grandchildren.

Thoughts to Ponder

from Cancer Doesn't Scare Me

1. God can override a doctor's prognosis.

2. Jesus still heals people today.

3. Stage 4 can be your best platform to proclaim Jesus.

If faced with a severe illness, how will you handle it?

Dear friend, I pray that you may enjoy good health and that all may go well with you, even as your soul is getting along well. — 3 John 1:2

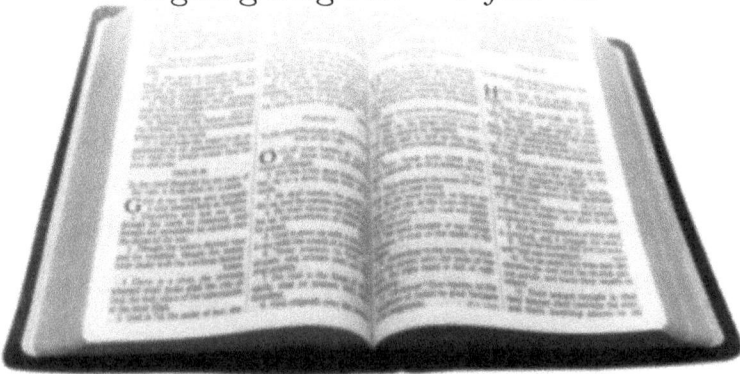

Facing a Bullet
by Lynne Russell

"Fearless."

That's what my close friends call me, and it's a word that best describes my personality.

I still wear a bracelet a friend gave me. It spells out f-i-e-r-c-e, another appropriate description, because I always possessed a desire to live on the wild side. For a while, that is exactly where I resided.

There's an additional word I want to share, "bullet" (a small metal projectile). A bullet changed the direction of my life as it ricocheted off the pavement in a small nook of an apartment complex. But I'll get back to that in a few.

I grew up in the Wild West, in the state of Wyoming. The oldest of three children, I was born fearless and in charge. I knew I could handle whatever came my way. Living in Wyoming made me tough as nails. I grew up hunting, not like they do in Texas (no offense meant to those who hunt in Texas), but hunting in Wyoming meant you got up very early and you tracked, walked, watched and shot. Then you quartered up the animal and packed it out. You did not do this on horseback. No squeamish, yuck, I can't handle the blood and guts, from this girl. You did it to survive.

I was a daddy's girl from the day I was born. One of my daddy's favorite things to tell me was "It's a big beautiful world. Go and get it!"

Another one of my favorite quotes is from James Dean. "Dream as though you will live forever; live as if you will die today."

Both of those were true for me. I dreamt about being invincible. Nothing could stop me, and I knew I would live forever. In reality, I always pushed the limit and could have died any day!

I have to share a bit of history before I take you on the adventure of my life. Born in the fifties, I was a teenager in the late sixties and early seventies. If you grew up at this time, it meant hippies, drugs, and murder. Who remembers what Charles Manson did in 1969? A reporter asked Charles Manson, "Who are you?" Charles Mason replied, "Nobody, I'm nobody. I'm a tramp, a bum, a hobo; I'm a boxcar, and a jug of wine, and a straight razor if you get close to me." He was a destructive force. Asked if he was Jesus Christ, Manson said, "Which one?" Manson said there are several: Black, Mexican, and Jewish. He said it's all in our mind. How bizarre to even think that way.

Needless to say, life in the sixties and seventies was different from today.

However, that was the decade of life that drew me to the destiny in my heart.

Growing up at that time, I loved watching the television show, "The Mod Squad," featuring Michael Cole as Pete, Peggy Lipton as Julie, and Clarence Williams II as Linc. I started dreaming about going into a line of work like the Mod Squad was in, police officers, who weekly engaged in exciting adventures as they fought crime. I wondered what it would be like to be Julie?

I saw many of my friends die from suicide, drug overdose and, yes, even murder.

So being the brave, fearless person I was born to be, I thought, *What can I do to stop the hurt, the trauma and the dying (a loss of spiritual life and end of life) of my family and friends.*

Lawyer? Nope, don't think so. Not so sure that is the best way to wipe out crime.

So I became Julie, a dream and an answer to help stop the ugliness. But that meant I had to become numb, and live in the ugliness. Filthy language, sex, drugs, and murder; all you can imagine it to be.

I was an undercover vice, narcotics and homicide detective. I thought, *Yep, now I can fight crime. I have a badge and a gun and I am fearless and ready to put the bad guys away.*

Back to the word, "Bullet." Remember the metal projectile? I was living recklessly. I was the big bad undercover detective. I could do anything on my own, with no help from anyone. And then, I found myself in a gun battle with an assailant. We were fighting over the gun and POW! The gun goes off. A bullet ricocheted (the motion of a projectile in rebounding or deflecting one or more times from the surface over which it is passing through, or against which it hits; a glancing blow).

As I watched the bullet bounce from wall-to-wall in slow motion, I witnessed something else. The Lord Jesus Christ appeared to me in full-blown glory. Looking at me He said, "Choose this day who ye will serve." I didn't think twice. Praise God, I chose Him, and then I watched the bullet plant itself in the body of my foe, killing him instantly. I wonder if Jesus asked him the same question?

The Lord saved my life on that day with the hand that bears the nail scars; He stopped the bullet! He met me right where I was, and reached His nail scarred, bullet-holed hand out to me. My life was never the same after that split-second happening with my Lord.

There was a dramatic change in me. I was still fearless, but fearless about my faith and family. Those were now my passion. Whether you believe in God or not, I believe we are called to walk beside family, friends and hurting people. Our brains are created to function in either fear or love, and the two cannot function in our brain at the same time. Love breaks down negativity and brings amazing things into our lives.

I now live out Romans 12:1-2, a passage that speaks about the sacrifice God wants us to make for him:

"Therefore, I urge you, brothers and sisters, in view of God's mercy, to offer your bodies as a living sacrifice, holy and pleasing to God—this is your true and proper worship. Do not conform to the pattern of this world, but be transformed by the renewing of your mind. Then you will be able to test and approve what God's will is—his good, pleasing and perfect will."

I chose Him in a split second, or I would have died and gone to hell. Unlike the culture around us, always dragging us down to its level of immaturity, after saying "yes" to Him, I found God brought out the best in me and developed well-formed maturity in my life.

When you surrender your life to Him, He will transform your life. He promises to never leave you nor forsake you!

My power and authority used to come from man. I had a badge, a gun and an attitude. I could do anything, and the world would have to listen. The temptations of the world blinded me. A gun and a badge were my power and authority. What was I thinking? Not anymore. I receive my power and authority from God.

I will end with a quote that expresses what the Lord has done for me. "Not all of us can be heroes; some of us have to be saved."

I thank the Lord every day he gave me that split second to choose Him. I thank the Lord He saved me. I pray you will also be fearless, and make the same choice. While you may never have a bullet staring you in the face, there is no guarantee there will be a tomorrow.

Lynne Russell is the co-author of a children's book, USELESS: A Donkey's Adventurous Tale. She also enjoyed a twenty-one year, award-winning career in television, radio, magazine, and newspaper media. Lynne is a certified Chaplin with The Church at Work and is also certified in Critical Incident Stress Management. Reach Lynne at lkayruss@gmail.com

Thoughts to Ponder
from Facing a Bullet

1. God always wants you to choose Him.

2. We do not know how long we have on this earth.

3. God often redirects our dreams.

Are you ready to meet your Maker?

Choose for yourselves this day
whom you will serve. Joshua 24:15

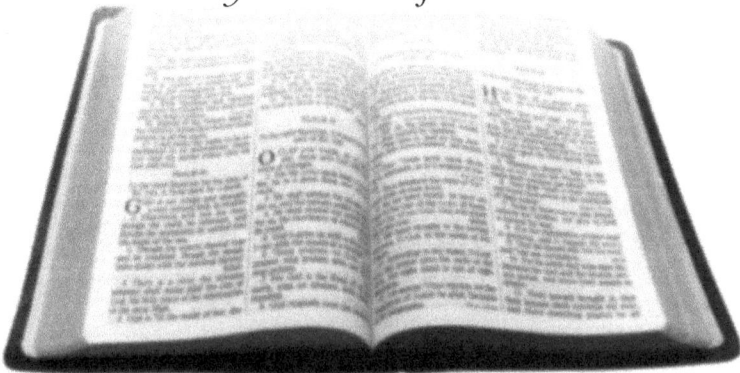

Chronicles of an Ex-Muslim
by Rabia Smith

Do you remember who your first love was?

The first person you ever had a crush on?

Or first time you thought you were in love?

Growing up, I was exposed to all sorts of romance movies and westerns. I fell in love with actor, Rock Hudson, at the tender age of eight. My plan was to come to America when I grew up and find Rock Hudson. He would take one look at me, and he would fall in love with me too. We would get married and live happily ever after. Oh, the imagination of a child!

While I never met Rock Hudson, I did realize my dream of coming to America. But first, I want to take you on a trip with me to my birthplace. Do you like to travel? We will fly over the oceans and seas to a continent called Africa, specifically to the Southern tip of Africa, South Africa, and to a town called Durban, the busiest port in South Africa.

I want to share about my early life so you can see how God's totally unearned forgiveness was evident in my life even before we officially "met."

I was conceived late in my parents' lives. My father was born in 1927, and my mother was born in 1939. I am the twelfth child out of thirteen. I grew up in a very religious Islamic household. My parents were devout Sunni Muslims. My family was, and still is, one of the religious leaders in our community. My mother founded a Madrasah (Islamic School) that was built on her property. Our day started very early. At 4 a.m., the entire neighborhood was awakened by the sound of a man singing in Arabic, over loud speakers. This singing is called the Adhan. Adhan is the call to prayer and all Muslim believers have to respond. This call to prayer invoked many feelings in me, including fear and pride.

This is what we'd hear over loud speakers:

Arabic: Allahu Akbar

English: God is Great. (x4)

Arabic: Ashhadu an la ilaha illa Allah

English: I bear witness that there is no god except the One God. (x2)

Arabic: Hayya 'ala-s-Salah

English: Hurry to the prayer. (Rise up for prayer) (x2)

Arabic: Hayya 'ala-l-Falah

English: Hurry to success. (Rise up for Salvation) (x2)

Arabic: Allahu Akbar

English: God is Great. (x2)

Arabic: La ilaha illa Allah

English: There is no god except the one God.

For the pre-dawn *(fajr)* prayer, the following phrase is inserted after the fifth part above, towards the end:

Arabic: As-salatu Khayrun Minan-nawm

English: Prayer is better than sleep. (x2)

One of my earliest memories was sitting on my mother's lap in Islamic school reciting the Quran, which is the Islamic sacred book. I remember coming to a particular Arabic phrase I could not remember. Each time I could not remember, I was beaten.

That was the day I realized I had to be perfect.

That was the day that fear became my foundation.

Besides having a strong religious background, there was also sexual and physical abuse in the household. I was angry and fearful, so I injected all my energy into schoolwork and became one of my mother's best students. There was constant chatter that I would continue this family legacy of my mother's ministry. My training as an Islamic Evangelist

34

began; but I still had many questions. The type of questions I asked were not encouraged.

Why was Allah so angry?

Why did He want to punish me?

I felt like Allah was an oppressive figure looming over me. Even though I was praying five times a day there was no comfort. Even though I felt all these things, I never entertained the thought that there was something apart from Islam. This was my life. Even when asked, "If you died today, where would go?" I would reply, "Hell." I knew I was Hell-bound. I accepted my fate.

Something was missing, but what?

My curious nature spilled over to other people. There was a lady that lived with us. She was a Zulu woman by the name of Bongisele. Every day Bongisele would take a black book that was wrapped in a red scarf off the shelf and read it. I would follow her around during the day. I asked her if she would teach me how to read Zulu from the black book she carefully wrapped daily. Our conversation went something like this:

Rabia: "Bongisele, please teach me to read Zulu."

Bongisele: "No. The madam would be angry if she saw you reading this book."

Rabia: "Please! I won't tell her. Teach me when she leaves."

I nagged her for weeks, then one afternoon when my mother left, Bongisele sat me in her lap and our lessons began. I was so excited! I could read Zulu. I didn't understand what I reading; I was just excited I was able to read Zulu. What I realized later is, I was reading the Bible. Bongisele planted the first seed.

In 1995, I fulfilled my dream of seeing the United States when I enrolled in college in the U.S. I was supposed to obtain a degree in nursing and return home after I completed my degree. My brother and sister-in-law already lived in the United States, so I was able to stay with them. In exchange for room and board, I babysat my niece (who had severe cerebral palsy) during the day and went to school at night. At one point my niece became very ill. I would watch her looking at other kids playing and I longed for her to be normal. My heart was breaking because I wanted her to be whole. I started praying extra prayers but she got worse.

One day, as I was sitting in front of the television flipping through channels, I remembered something my mother taught me. She said, "It is permissible to accept prayer from a Jew or a Christian because they are people of the book." I stumbled upon *The 700 Club*. I dialed the number that was scrolling at the bottom of the screen. A woman answered the phone and I said to her, "Look I know you Christians talk about being born again, but I don't need your Jesus. I need you to pray for my niece who is sick." The woman prayed, and something happened. I could not comprehend the presence I felt. It was strange, yet peaceful. I felt like I was wrapped in a bubble. I was there, but was I?

What happened was nothing like I ever imagined. I realized that Jesus could be more than just a Prophet. (In Islam, Jesus is revered as one of the Major Prophets.) I remained in a state of confusion and turmoil for eight years. Could my entire life be a lie? I kept asking myself, "How could this be?" I didn't know who I was anymore. I had to find out. However, I was afraid to denounce Islam because of my family. Fear and loyalty had been imputed into me. As I child I would always say, "I was born a Muslim and I'll die a Muslim." I struggled to wrap my head around the fact that Jesus was God. It was against everything I was ever taught. Deep down, I knew that Jesus was more special than what I was taught. He just felt right. But fear had a stronger hold. This was the beginning of my spiritual journey.

In June of 2006, I had another experience with God when he revealed Proverbs, 3:5-6 to me in a vision. Proverbs 3:5-6 says, "Trust in the LORD with all your heart and lean not on your own understanding; in all your ways submit to him, and he will make your paths straight."

There was no more doubt. I believed with all my heart. I wanted the world to know about my newfound faith; so on June 13, 2006, I was baptized.

My life changed drastically after I was born again. Was it a smooth transition? Absolutely not. Was my family accepting of my conversion? No, they were not. During the early years, did I ever consider going back to Islam? No, I never entertained that thought. You see, God became a very close companion and real to me. He delighted in me. I did not know much back then, but I was certain of one thing, He loved me. I had never experienced a love like this. He was always near. We were in constant fellowship. I fell madly and deeply in love.

I began to meditate on the Word of God and my mindset changed. I understood my rights in Christ. I became Christ conscious and knew my identity. My mind was renewed. The fear that bound me my entire life left me. I knew who I was and the more I studied the Word, the stronger I became. The Word took root in my Spirit. I began to eat the Word veraciously. My thirst for the Word became unquenchable. I simply cannot get enough.

One of my favorite scriptures is Hebrews 4:12, "That the Word of God is alive and active, sharper than any two edged sword, it penetrates even to dividing soul and spirit, joints and marrow; it judges the thoughts and attitudes of the heart." This Scripture really touches me deeply. You see no matter what walk of life you come from or what your past looks like, you are now a new creation in Christ. This Word of God, builds, breaks, removes, cleans, fixes, empowers, transforms and molds you into who God says you are. When this Word gets into your spirit, remnants of your past will not be visible. Your life becomes a wonder. No longer will you be bound by the opinion of man. The Word of God establishes you. I am unashamedly in love. A woman after God's own heart, just like King David from the Bible. I would change nothing, irrespective of all the relationships I've lost. I've gained so much more. I am complete in Him.

My story is a love story that I must share, because it's about an enduring, eternal love, so much deeper than any schoolgirl crush. The love I receive from God is more fulfilling than my faith background could provide and I am thankful he introduced himself to me.

What about you? Do you desire a love greater than you can imagine? Then ask God to reveal his love to you. That's the beautiful thing about the Lord. He has more than enough love to cover the globe, from America to Africa, and anywhere in between.

Rabia Smith is a woman who is after God's own heart. She is a native of Durban, South Africa and has made Dallas, Texas her home. Rabia is a former Muslim. Her passion is for the lost and to empower believers to live victorious lives through the Word of God.

Thoughts to Ponder
from Chronicles of an Ex-Muslim

1. There is only one way to God.

2. God wants all to come to Him through Jesus, His Son.

3. God uses media to reach people.

With whom do you need to share the Gospel?

He is patient with you, not wanting anyone to perish, but everyone to come to repentance. — 2 Peter 3:9

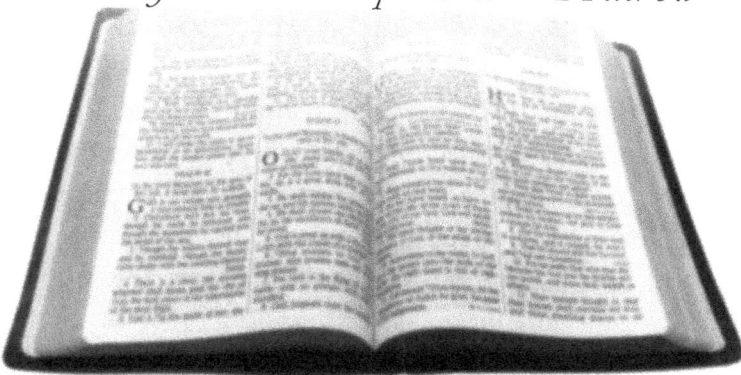

Charlie's Angels

by Shannon Virginia Johnson

"Good morning, Angels! Time to get to work!"

Those words changed my life in January 1976 when the television show, "Charlie's Angels," debuted on American television. Farrah Fawcett, Jacquelyn Smith, and Kate Jackson were sophisticated, beautiful, athletic, and inquisitive. The Angels were private investigators with sleek sleuthing skills, and I wanted to be just like them when I grew up. My cousins and I played Charlie's Angels all the time, and we even practiced our perfect Farrah Fawcett feathered bangs in the mirror.

Every episode of Charlie's Angels had a villain, a mystery to solve, and a carefully crafted investigative plan. The Angels employed three investigative tools, which private investigators still use today—researching public records, conducting surveillance on individuals to learn about their behavior, and interviewing individuals with relevant information. If my life were an episode of Charlie's Angels, it would be titled, "HUSH!" The villain is an identity thief, because he's tried to silence me through shame and the circumstances of three big events in my life.

The episode of my life opens with a little girl who had an incurable curiosity and loved to ask everyone questions. When I asked my grandmother if Juicy Fruit really grew on trees like it did in the Wrigley's commercials of the 1970's, she smiled and gently replied, "Oh, hush up." When I asked my mother to explain why my pet rock never moved, the rolling of her eyes silenced me. I grew up in a more formal setting, and quickly learned I was to be seen, but not heard. We were to put on our mask and smile as if everything was always perfect. Ironically, I grew up in the church and did religion very well, but I completely missed the most important part, having a personal relationship with Jesus Christ.

I mastered looking the part, but I was hollow inside and felt counterfeit. I was easily intimidated and silenced by the wealth of Bible knowledge, scripture memorized by other Christians, and how they could hear God. I thought I had to understand everything before I could believe, but at the age of 23, I realized I simply had to believe so I might understand. I stepped out of religion and into relationship when I invited Jesus into my heart. I began to feel authentic, find my voice, and gain the confidence that comes through a true identity in Christ.

In "HUSH!" that young woman continues to grow up, but the villain always lurked in the shadows behind her.

Every little girl dreams of planning her wedding, and when I was 28, I began to plan mine. A month after my spring engagement, my mother was diagnosed with terminal ovarian cancer. I dreamed of planning my wedding with my mother for years, but she was too ill to help. My father lovingly stepped in as "Frank Banks," the wedding planner from the movie "Father of the Bride." We spent the summer together, making all kinds of bridal decisions. We met joy at every turn and conspired for me to surprise my mother by wearing her wedding dress. Little did we know we were not only planning my wedding, but we were also planning my father's going away party. My wedding day was the last day I saw my father, for he died unexpectedly three weeks later during a March of Dimes Walk. I remember calling family and friends to tell them this news, and they thought I misspoke: "You mean your mother?" "No," I said. "My father."

Months later, my mother passed away. Even though I welcomed the new roles of wife and expectant mother, I had not bargained for my new role as an orphan. The identity thief had a field day. In losing my parents, I lost a sense of identity in the world, and my identity in Christ faded, too. I felt abandoned and was silenced by aloneness, which feels very different from loneliness.

But God, in His great love and compassion for us, meets us right where we are. When my sisters and I planned our father's memorial service, we sought the family Bible. As I pulled the Bible off the shelf, a mauve-colored greeting card envelope fell out of the pages. Curious, I picked the envelope up and we noticed it was sealed. There was no writing on the outside of the envelope either. My youngest sister nudged me to open the envelope. Tucked inside was a greeting card, and here's what it said on the front: "If it hurts you to look behind . . ." On the inside it read, "And it frightens you to look ahead, just look beside you and I'll be there." There was no signature! We still refer to that greeting card as our Hallmark from heaven.

During this season of grief, loss and abandonment, I researched and read some wonderful Christian books, but I still felt silenced by the weight of abandonment. Like a good Charlie's Angel, I went straight to the source and used my sleuthing skills to research God's Word. As I poured over the scriptures, tears stained the pages, and abandonment melted away. I discovered a relationship with God the Father, who will never leave me nor forsake me. Like that heaven-sent greeting card promised, I just look to my side, and my Father God is always there. Always.

Life moved forward in joy, and I gave birth to three children; but the villain was still on the loose. I turned forty and was hoping to coast in life a little bit. We were on summer vacation in Montana when I was busy picking up the kids' dirty clothes and shoes from a day of hiking. My arms full, one of the Keen shoes pressed into my neck, and it was painful. I dropped everything to reach for my neck, and that's when I felt a golf ball-sized lump tucked at the base of my neck. I reached around the base of my neck to discover a series of rock-hard lumps. I knew immediately I had lymphoma like our pet, a German short hair pointer named Chief, at home. You see, all year our dog had been suffering from lymphoma, and I knew from petting him what cancer felt like.

Ironically, when we returned home from vacation, Chief had to be put down the same day I was diagnosed with stage three Anaplastic, Large T-cell Non-Hodgkin's lymphoma. To me, that was just a fancy name for fear and death.

This type of lymphoma is one of the most aggressive kinds, so the fight was up front. I was prescribed six rounds of chemotherapy, and I put my game face on. What complicated this battle was the identity thief's tactic, convincing me I would die from cancer just like my mom. I realized I buried my grief for her in the busyness of motherhood. Paralyzed by fear and gripped by death, everything I did reminded me of her, the smell of the chemotherapy and the infusion room, doctor visits, chilly hospital halls, buying a wig and my bald head.

One of the medicines in the chemo cocktail was nicknamed "the red devil" because it loved hair. For a woman, her hair is part of her history, especially in the south where I grew up. In my own life, I can recall having the Dorothy Hamill haircut in elementary school before I perfected the Farrah Fawcett feathered bangs. During high school, my Princess Diana bi-level cut gave in to the Madonna "Material Girl" look. Then there was the short Republican bob of the early 1990's. Cancer stole my favorite hairstyle, the ponytail of motherhood.

Losing your hair to disease has nothing to do with vanity, but everything to do with feeling vulnerable and exposed. You cannot hide from the disease when the mirror reflects your bare head right back to you; nor could I hide cancer from my young children. Sometimes my bald head felt like a beacon for pity or a ticket to stare. The villain took advantage of this opportunity, and turned my baldness into a hopelessness that hushed my heart.

I bought a wig because I thought I was supposed to, and the kids nicknamed it "Madge." I tried to wear Madge, but it was very uncomfortable. During this time, my aunts presented me with a basket full of my grandmother's scarves, which she had collected on her travels. I shelved Madge and wore those scarves daily. Each scarf felt like a hug from heaven. The colorful scarves comforted me and made me feel safe. The kids loved to pick out which scarf I should wear, and they helped me tie them on as if placing a helmet of salvation from God's armor on my head.

During this time my oldest son attended Cotillion with his fellow fifth graders at the San Antonio Country Club. It was the last night when fathers accompany their daughters and mothers, their sons. I was in my closet getting ready for my big date with Colton when he came in. He stood in the doorway as I asked him which scarf I should wear. Colton was silent, and he could not look at me. My chin quivering, I understood what he couldn't say. He was embarrassed, and wishing I looked like all the other moms that night.

So I said, "Colton, why don't we take Madge out on the dance floor tonight and give her a whirl!" His face lit up, and he looked me in the eye. "YES!" I put Madge on and brushed her blonde hair, but no matter how I styled her hair, I could not cover up the wide seam in the front. It was impossible to wear Madge alone, so I had to wear a black hat on top of the wig. I confess I felt uncomfortable and more like the mysterious imposter that occasionally appeared on

"Days of Our Lives," the soap opera that generations have watched in my family.

Colton and I had the time of our lives as we waltzed to George Strait, but what I didn't anticipate was how hard it would be to take that wig off when I got home. I changed clothes and paused in the mirror, pretending everything was normal, like the beginning of that summer vacation. I slowly pulled Madge off, and I crumpled to the floor.

That's when I heard my Father God say, "Do not live by what you see. Live by Me." You see, I had been doing surveillance on all the wrong things to determine my survival—test results, statistics, circumstances, that silly bald head, worry written on my friends' faces, my mother's outcome. Like a good Charlie's Angel, I needed to do surveillance on what really mattered, so I began to do surveillance on Jesus Christ and His behavior, what the life of Christ looked like and what it meant to live life *through* Christ.

A friend of mine made a prayer appointment at Christ Healing Center, a non-denominational, Christ-centered house of prayer in San Antonio. We gathered for prayer and returned weekly with more friends to pray. Psalm 144:1 says, "The Lord God my Rock trains my hands for war, my fingers for battle." I warred with my hands in prayer and learned the power of praying in the Name of Jesus. I got mad, not at God, but at the villain who was stealing my hope and my health. I was not going to let the identity thief silence me through fear nor hold me captive to death anymore. Focusing on life in Christ healed my heart and restored my hope.

After the third round of chemo, it was time to do a CT scan to see if the tumors had shrunk or determine if we need to change the treatment plan. My doctor called me and said, "What have you been doing?" I said, "What do you mean?"

She triumphantly declared, "The cancer is gone! It's absolutely gone. There is not a trace of lymphoma. What have you been doing?" "Prayer." She sighed and said, "Well don't stop!"

This was a miraculous healing that defied the medical team. I don't understand why I experienced healing here on earth while others may go to heaven to be healed. That is part of the mystery of the Lord we can never understand, but I do know healing always takes place, no matter the outcome. I met God the Father, but now I knew God the Son and how a life in Christ always yields the healing heart, the healing hand and a healing hope through the resurrection power of Jesus Christ to make all things new.

The episode "HUSH!" continues. What I did not fully appreciate at that time were the blessings I received from journeying with cancer. Having to fight for my life transformed into a holy boldness, and my hushed spirit turned into a voice that would soon soar. These gifts prepared me for the identity thief's third and lowest blow. Disease happens. Death happens. But what happened next was by choice, and that felt like a gut punch.

Two days before our family's spring break trip to Belize, I awoke from a dream. In this dream, my husband left early in the morning for his workout class, like he did every day at 4:30 a.m. in real life. I looked to my right, and there's Jesus. He was wearing a white robe, and I was struck by how big the bell sleeve near His wrist was as He motioned for me to follow Him. Then we began walking diagonally across a concrete courtyard in a red-bricked apartment complex. I could hear the hem of His robe catching the concrete as he led me to a door. Jesus stepped behind me and gently nudged me forward to knock on the door. I looked back at Jesus to make sure I should knock and perhaps for some holy boldness, too. Silently, He nodded. So I knocked. A young, beautiful girl in her twenties answered the door and was very obviously shocked to see me. Jesus nudged me forward, and we walked further into the apartment. That's when I saw three more girls in the apartment who were just as surprised to see me. None of them saw Jesus standing to my right, my Rock. The doorbell rang, and the young girl opened the door to my husband. There he was in his workout clothes and eager to come on in. I couldn't see what the girl was telling him with her facial expressions, but it was obvious from his reaction she was telling him it was not a good time and to return later. With his arms like exclamation marks punctuating his impatience, he grew angry, "What do you mean I can't come in? I come here all the time!" That's when I looked over to Jesus, questioning Him with my eyes. I'll never forget the grief and sorrow on His face as He closed His eyes, tucking His chin near His heart. I knew what He was showing me—adultery.

Like God in His great love and mercy for His children, the dream did not end there. The scene changed, and I was walking with Jesus. He was in step right beside me. The sun was brilliant and shining, reflecting its golden glory on the water to our left. We walked in joy along the wide sidewalk that followed the water. I was overcome with that peace that surpasses all understanding, the kind when words get caught in your throat as you try to describe it. As we walked silently, Jesus extended His right arm out and across His chest. The bell sleeve hanging from His wrist caught my attention again. He looked over to me, smiled and exclaimed, "This is where I am taking you. This is where you shall live."

I woke up from that dream with a heavy heart. I suspected infidelity in my marriage for over a decade, but I could never prove anything. After each time I suspected something, then time would pass. I would tell myself it was all my imagination, and that I was crazy for thinking my husband was unfaithful. But this dream felt different, like a warning, a revelation. I was silenced like the calm that anticipates a storm. I could feel the storm coming, but I decided to focus on the end of that dream and the promise of that Hallmark card from years before, Jesus would be right beside me no matter what.

A few days later after dinner in Belize, my daughter came bouncing over to me and asked me who a certain woman's name was. I told her I didn't know and asked, "Why?" She said, "I was just wondering because daddy's been emailing her and texting her a lot on our family vacation." I felt a lightning bolt of truth pierce my spirit from head to toe. Now the dream made sense, and I wasn't crazy after all for suspecting infidelity during my marriage.

We returned home, and I discovered unfaithfulness to various degrees throughout our marriage and uncovered financial funny business, too. Your body and health may betray you, but this betrayal was by choice, again and again and again. That kind of betrayal was the hardest to accept from my beloved. Everything I thought to be true was turned inside out, upside down.

The identity thief worked overtime and employed his cruelest tactics, holding me captive to the lies and false identity that I was not enough, I was not pretty enough, I was not sexy enough, I was unlovable, I was rejected, I was unworthy, I was my husband's inconvenience, and I was a failure and a fool. Those lies had been creeping in for years and finally hushed me into the silence of shame. When I filed for divorce, and the villain used the stigma of divorce and shame to isolate me from friends and church, he crucified my confidence, too.

During this time, sleep was hard to come by. I began waking up every morning at 3:33 a.m. I would happen to catch 3:33 p.m. on the clock in carpool line. I admit I was irritated because I had usually just fallen asleep before 3:33 a.m. Finally, I realized there must be some significance to 3:33 a.m., so the next morning I asked God at 3:34 a.m., "What are you trying to tell me?" I heard the word "Jeremiah." So I looked in my Bible for Jeremiah 3:33, but there's no such verse. Then He led me to Jeremiah 33:3, which says: "Call unto Me, and I will answer you and tell you great and unsearchable things which you do not know."

You see, like a good Charlie's Angel, I interviewed lawyers, counselors, pastors, private investigators, and forensic accountants to glean relevant information for my divorce; but I had neglected to interview the most important person—God. He did not say He might answer me, but God said, "Call unto Me, and I will answer you." I began to interview God through prayer for all things, and it was during this time I was introduced to God, the Holy Spirit, who comforts us, counsels us and gives us truth. It was like the Lord would take hold of my hand, look at me and say," Today I am going to reveal some truth to you. It may hurt, but trust Me."

As 2 Corinthians 3:17 says, "Now the Lord is Spirit, and where the Spirit of the Lord is, there is freedom." The truth of my marriage and our finances was revealed like rapid fire in the smallest details, and the more I learned, the freer I felt. Yes, Truth set me free. Most importantly, the Holy Spirit set me free with the truth of Psalm 34:5, which lovingly declares, "Those who look to Him are radiant; their faces are never covered with shame." Did you hear that? Those who look to Christ are radiant. Their faces are never covered with shame!

At the end of every Charlie's Angel episode, the villain is caught and the mystery is solved. At the end of my life's episode "HUSH!", the villain tried to silence me and steal my identity through the circumstances of death, disease and divorce. Claiming the authority of God the Father, the name of God the Son, Jesus Christ, and the power of God the Holy Spirit, I hushed the enemy once and for all. After the divorce, I moved to Dallas and became a certified private investigator, fulfilling my childhood dream of being a Charlie's Angel.

The villain would love to hush us up and hold us captive to a false identity, trapped and tormented by the lies of abandonment, death, shame, and you're not enough. Colossians 2:6–8 says, "So then, just as you received Christ Jesus as Lord, continue to live your lives in Him, rooted and built up in Him, strengthened in the faith as you were taught, and overflowing with thankfulness. See to it that no one takes you captive through hollow and deceptive philosophy, which depends on human tradition and the elemental spiritual forces of this world rather than on Christ."

Like Charlie's Angels, we have an investigative plan to catch this thief. We can practice using a private investigator's techniques, research God's Word, do surveillance on the life of Christ, and interview God through prayer. In other words, know that God the Father will never leave you nor forsake you, keep your eyes fixed on Jesus and always seek Him first. And just like Charlie told his Angels at the close of every episode, the Lord will tell you, "Good work, Angels!"

Shannon Johnson is a chaplain, private investigator, speaker and a writer. As a human trafficking advocate, she uses these skills to search for missing and exploited minors. Shannon is passionate about esteeming, equipping and establishing women in Christ, too. She lives in Dallas and has three teenagers.

Thoughts to Ponder
from Charlie's Angels

1. God works with the desires of your heart.

2. God wants us to lean on Him through our trials.

3. Christ gives us strength in our weakness.

What childhood dream would you still like to pursue?

Consider it joy . . . whenever you face trials of many kinds, because you know that the testing of your faith produces perseverance. — James 1:2–4

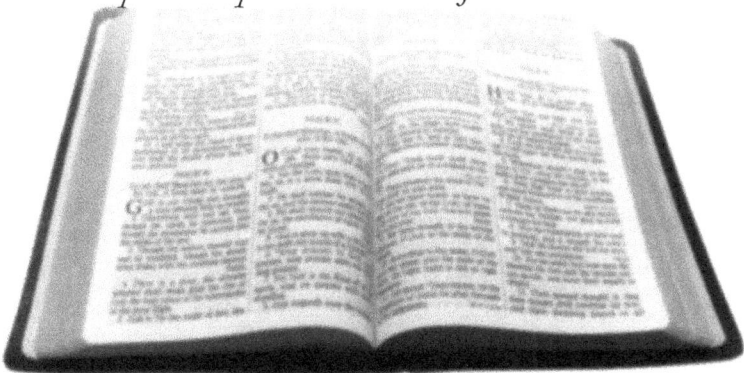

The Tragic Call
by Sharon Fox

My husband and I are deciding if we should keep our landline or go with our cell phones only. It would be lovely to be rid of the telemarketers who congratulate us by saying: "You have won a three day trip to Las Vegas" or the dinnertime calls wanting an opinion on a political issue. Think with me for a moment about phone calls of another nature, ones that changed your pathway in life. It's a phone call that creates an unexpected detour or a change of trajectory. Perhaps you can recall one of those "detour" calls.

Was it a call from the Human Resource office directing you to attend a personal meeting with the head of the department at 3:30 on Friday afternoon?

Or a call from the doctor's office, stating that although your appointment is next Tuesday, the test results are back, and the doctor wants to see you tomorrow morning?

Or perhaps a call from a brother or sister that went like this: "I am at the hospital with Nana. Things are bad. You need to come as soon as you can."

Or from your son or daughter. "Mom, Dad, I am at the police station. I am in trouble. Can you come down here and help me?"

I had such a call. My call was on a Wednesday night just after 11 p.m. when I found out my sister was murdered. It was first reported as a home invasion. The authorities thought it was a robbery that went terribly wrong. My sister was beaten and stabbed, and there were signs of a break-in. This call rocked my world.

I labeled myself a Christian for as long as I could remember. Upon reflection, I believe the best way to state my relationship with God was a "one toe over the line"

Christian. I attended church regularly and was active in church activities. Yet I had a shallow trust in God and was missing a deep relationship with Jesus.

All the classic symptoms of grief overwhelmed me during the weeks and months that followed the call. I suffered stomach pain, and was angry and difficult to be around as the details of the murder unfolded. Ten days after my sister's death, police arrested my brother-in-law for my sister's murder.

I felt deep sadness.

I felt betrayed by my brother-in-law, who had been a part of the family for thirty-five years, yet killed my sister.

I also felt betrayed by God.

How could He let this happen to my sister? She was the deeply rooted Christian I strived to be. She was an honest, authentic Christian.

I recall standing at the kitchen sink, with my hand on my hip, saying out loud, "God, were you not paying attention? What happened to faithfully protecting her? Did you blink when this terrible thing happened to my sister?"

A few months after my sister's death, I signed up for a grief recovery class at my church. It was the first one ever offered. I learned many things over the weeks of the course. The first night, I cried uncontrollably for two hours. I went home and told my family. "I am in real trouble. I don't know how to grieve, and I am so mad." I was given permission that night to say out loud, "I am angry with my brother-in-law, and I am angry at GOD!"

Anger, I learned, is a normal reaction in many grief related situations, but I developed my own brand of anger. I allowed anger to become the centerpiece of my being. I call it "smoldering rage." As a Christian woman, I thought I was not allowed to get mad. So, I buried the deep hurt, anger, and sadness, and it became toxic. It permeated every part of my being. Physically, this anger manifested in my body through stomach issues and headaches. Emotionally, I cried a lot. Spiritually, I questioned my trust in God. Intellectually, I strived to think clearly at work.

However, through the grief training, I learned about the free will God gives us. He loves us so much we get to choose to love him, or choose to reject him. We can choose right from wrong. My brother-in-law used his free will to choose. He chose a sinful life that resulted in the murder of my sister. But the greatest lesson I learned was about God's faithfulness that could only be seen through thankful eyes.

God's faithfulness was unfailing in the early days after my sister's murder. The night of the murder, an investigator reported to the house immediately after the 911 call. The investigator had recently completed an intense training session on evidence gathering. His observation at the crime scene, combined with the evidence found the next morning, led to the arrest. He collected "red flags," as he called them, when he arrived at the crime scene. The officer took notice of the way my brother-in-law was dressed, his emotional state, and how he responded to questions. When it was time for his statement to be taken, the investigator spotted inconsistencies in the story as well. Details gathered that night prompted the officer to dig deeper into the suspicious story my brother-in-law fabricated.

The investigator displayed his best work when he asked my brother-in-law to retrace his activities from the night before. He noted times and distances, and checked them against the building logs where he said he was during the murder. The investigator noticed a dumpster behind the office building where my brother-in-law worked. He called the crime lab to have the dumpster picked up and processed at a secure location. The crime lab found a plastic bag in the dumpster, the evidence that later was the basis of the conviction. The dumpster was not picked up by a trash hauler the night of the murder, as it normally would have been. The driver called in sick. That dumpster would have been sent to a landfill. The mother lode of the evidence would have been lost forever. They found the knife, pipe, the stolen items, and five rubber gloves containing fingerprints of my brother-in-law, as well as my sister's blood on the gloves. Many of those details were not disclosed to my family for almost a year.

God protected the evidence, and he prompted the investigator to carefully evaluate and investigate the observable details of the case.

The court date was set three times before it finally began in October, two-and-a-half years after my sister's death. About six months prior to the final trial date, I prayed with other members of my family five nights a week at 10 p.m. It was during those nightly prayer times that I began to be thankful for what God had done. I saw with thankful eyes His amazing provision and faithfulness. In our prayers, we always included the judge, (we did not know who it would be, but God did), the jury panel, (again, they were not selected until two days before the trial began, but God knew who they were), those who would testify, and for the two state employed prosecutors who presented the case. They were men of faith who worked hard to present the evidence in a compelling way.

My brother-in-law spent two million dollars for his defense. There were seven attorneys in the courtroom every day. They rolled in stacks of file boxes of "evidence" every day as a backdrop to the attorney's presence. If you know the story of David and Goliath, the big guys against the little guys; that was the courtroom drama.

At the end of the trial, my brother-in-law was found guilty and sentenced to thirty-two years in prison. He is still in prison. God's hands of protection were all over the investigation, the courtroom testimony, and the verdict.

The impact of my grief recovery class did not end after six weeks. In those weeks I learned new coping skills to deal with anger. I learned that my choice not to forgive my brother-in-law was crushing me. I had to forgive to be content again. I knew if God forgives me of my sins, through the gift of Jesus who sacrificed His life for me, I needed to forgive others too.

I have been inspired to look further into the lessons of grief. One of the leaders of the grief class said, "Sharon came to class, and she never went home." As I researched writings on grief, I found most of the material up to that time was secular in nature. You may know the name Elizabeth Kubler-Ross, who wrote groundbreaking materials on grief. Her work, however, was with people in hospitals who were dying, not with the survivors of a tragic loss. The "God understands your grief experience, because He felt grief too, because his son, Jesus, died," was not being shared with those who grieved. The concept of God's comfort and faithfulness was missing.

Because of that, I began a grief recovery ministry that has been a part of my life for almost twenty years. I have shared God's model of grieving with thousands of grieving people who have suffered losses such as the death of parents, a child, spouse, experiencing a miscarriage, divorce, job loss, death of a beloved pet, illness, and the impact of addiction and abortion. I am certified as a Grief Facilitator. I have spoken at national conferences and written two Christian based books on grief. The Bible says, "And we know that in all things God works for the good of those who love him, who have been called according to his purpose" (Romans 8:28). I, to my utter surprise, was called.

God is faithful. I see his faithfulness with thankful eyes. I am thankful for the driver who did not come to work, as the evidence would have been lost. I am thankful for the recent training the investigator had just taken. I am thankful for the jury who listened and discerned the evidence to determine the verdict. I am thankful that I have forgiven my brother-in-law and do not carry the burden of un-forgiveness. I am thankful for the peace that I live out every day. I am thankful that when you and I feel abandoned, angry, sad, loaded up with guilt and resentment, or any other negative emotion, God can change all that. He can be glorified in the midst of the most awful circumstances.

Imagine for a moment there is another call, but this time it's for you. It is an open line to God. He is waiting to hear from you because, like me, he may want to use your story to change the trajectory of your life. There will always be tragedy in our lives, and God knows the way to turn something tragic into good, if we are willing to let Him work through us. It's time to pick up the phone and listen.

Sharon Fox is an author, speaker and co-founder of Brave Penny (non-profit) and a certified Grief Facilitator. Her books, Reframing Adoption and A Precious Loss, reflect her heart for those who struggle with loss. Her third book, The Stone Carver Son, is a Christian Christmas book for children.

Thoughts to Ponder

from The Tragic Call

1. Life can be unpredictable.

2. Grief is a God-given emotion.

3. We must forgive what seems unforgivable.

How have you felt God's presence during your grief process?

But if you do not forgive others their sins,
your Father will not forgive your sins.
— Matthew 6:15

Bullied to Beloved
by Elizabeth Broz

On April 20, 1999, two teenage boys walked into Columbine High School and randomly shot their classmates. Like most Americans, my husband and I were glued to our television set, watching and re-watching the horrific scenes. At some point, my husband said, "How in the world do two teenage boys get to a point where something like this makes sense?" I looked over at him and said, "I know exactly how you can come to that place and feel justified in what you are doing."

In order to understand why I would respond that way, I need to take you back to when I was in middle school, which, in my school district was fifth through eighth grade. I was a typical young girl in many ways. I came from a loving, two-parent home in a middle class neighborhood in southern New Jersey. We attended church, had a loving extended family, and I felt loved and secure.

I was a bright kid, but shy and introverted. I felt different from other kids, kind of a square peg. And on top of all that, I was unattractive. I had a lazy eye that stayed over to the side. I wore glasses, and I was born with a jaw abnormality, causing my mouth to not close properly and hang open. I appeared to have buckteeth. As you can imagine, I took a good deal of teasing about my appearance.

The first memory that stands out happened one morning while riding the bus to school. A girl sitting across from me called my name. When I looked over, she stared out the window with her mouth hanging open and had a goofy look on her face. At first, I didn't understand what she was doing, but she was making fun of me. She did it several times, and I ignored her. One of the boys on the bus was watching her, laughing. He stood up, pointed at me, and said, "She's such a dog face," and then starting barking. Other boys joined in, and from that day on, every bus ride was a nightmare.

Literally, every day I listened to comments all the way to and from school.

"Does your face hurt, because it's killing me."

"Is every mirror in your house broken, because you looked in it?"

"Why don't you just stay home so we don't have to look at you every day?"

I dreaded getting on the bus every morning and every afternoon for most of my middle school years. But during the school day, it was even worse because classmates made fun of me several times a day. I walked into a classroom, and the boys started barking or making some loud comment about my appearance. It was usually three or four of them. Thankfully, not everyone joined in. Sometimes they snatched my homework and ripped it up, so I couldn't turn it in. They shoved me, knocked books out of my hands, and did anything to harass me. I pretended not to notice, but I felt humiliated. I think some of the girls felt badly about it, but they didn't stand up for me. I honestly think they just didn't know what to do. I desperately wanted someone to support me, but it rarely happened. My teachers were aware of the situation too, but most just ignored it. I don't think they knew what to do either. Some of my male teachers actually encouraged the behavior by laughing at the comments or letting them bark at me. It was awful.

When I was in fifth grade, I had a male English teacher. He assigned projects in the class that required us to go to the library and do research. On certain days, our teacher would allow us to use classroom time to go to the library. He would allow two students at a time to go for fifteen minutes. If we wanted to go, we would write our names on the chalkboard, and after he called our names to go, he would erase those two names so he'd know who was next. Several times through the year when my name was on the board, he erased it and acted like it was never there. He'd actually looked at me and smirked, like he was waiting for a reaction. I wanted so badly to say something, but I was timid and fearful. I was sure no one would have my back, even if I were brave enough to stand up for myself.

As time went on, I began to feel extremely insecure. I was embarrassed about the way I looked. I had no self-esteem or self-confidence. I assumed that everyone I met looked at me in disgust. Over time, I became angry and vengeful. I remember the first time I had a violent, angry thought. I was in seventh grade, and the Farrah Fawcett hairdo was all the rage. It seemed every girl in school had some version of that hairstyle. Most of the girls in my area of New Jersey were either of Italian or Jewish decent, so they had thick, wavy hair that seemed to be perfect for "the Farrah." I had the straightest hair you can imagine. Even with a curling iron, I couldn't get those flips. On the weekend, I figured out if I rolled my hair in those spongy pink rollers and wore them to bed, I could get those flips! I was so excited. My friend's dad even said my hair looked pretty the first time I did it. I thought, *Finally, I'll look like everybody else.*

So I went to school on Monday, nervous, not sure what people would think. Everyone noticed, but no one said anything, which was actually better, because I reached the point where I didn't want to be singled out for anything, good or bad. That day, we had a test in English class, so everyone was sitting quietly, working. In the middle of the test, with no provocation, the boy sitting directly across from me leans over and whispers to me, "You think you look pretty just because of your hair, don't you? Well you don't. You're still ugly and always will be."

Suddenly, I felt heat rising in my body; my heart began to pound, and I felt numb. I visualized leaning over and stabbing him in the stomach with a knife. I told myself the next day I would bring a knife to school, and as soon as he opened his mouth, he was getting it. I honestly believed he deserved it; he needed to pay for the way he treated me all these years. I never brought a knife to school, but after that day, I began to have murderous thoughts all the time. Thoughts of throwing burning sticks, soaked in gasoline, into my tormentors' bedrooms, burning down their houses; thoughts of stabbing people in the middle of the classroom so everyone would see it, and know that I was not going to put up with their constant teasing anymore. "You tease me; you pay!" The scary part is I felt completely justified in those thoughts. While I never acted on them, I honestly felt that if I had, they deserved it. *Who gave them the right to make my life so miserable?* So I can understand how Eric Harris and Dylan Klebold, the Columbine murderers, became enraged. I never acted on that anger, but internalized it, which began years of self-hatred and a feeling of worthlessness.

When high school started, things settled down a bit. I think people naturally grew up a little more at that age, so the bullying was not as intense. I made a few friends, hanging out with a group of people in my neighborhood. I also smoked pot and partied a lot, but I felt that I was having fun for the first time in my life. I did fit in somewhere. Then, at the end of ninth grade, my dad announced he was taking a job in Houston, and we would be moving as soon as the school year ended. I was devastated! I finally had friends, and now I was going to have to start all over again. But after thinking about the move, I thought it could be a good thing. I would have an opportunity to get a new reputation, just the new girl in school, not the ugly girl that everyone knew from middle school. Maybe people would finally see *me*, not my appearance.

So, on the first day of school in Houston during my sophomore year, I got on the bus to go to school. I sat alone, not knowing anyone. A few minutes into the bus ride, the two boys sitting across from me starting pointing and laughing. I don't remember exactly what they said, but they were making fun of me and teasing me about my appearance. I remember feeling utterly humiliated. I leaned my head against the window and decided right then and there that my life would never be different. I would always be the ugly girl that no one wanted around. I literally felt all hope leave me that day. My heart was heavy, and I felt empty. I decided I would turn off my feelings. I would never allow myself to feel anything again. That's how I would protect myself.

My personality changed after that. I acted awkward and weird. I did things I knew would make people reject me, but I couldn't help myself. I didn't know why I was acting that way, but I couldn't seem to do anything about it. I began taking drugs and had no motivation in life. I worked part time, still made good grades, and had a few good friends, but I was emotionally disengaged. I was afraid to step out and try anything new, for fear it would give people even more ammunition to tease me or put me down. I was intelligent; I could have done anything with my life that I wanted to, but was paralyzed with fear. I thought if I made a single mistake or did anything that wasn't perfect, everyone around me would talk about me or laugh at me, so I did nothing at all. I existed, but I had no life in me.

In the summer between my junior and senior year, I underwent surgery to fix my jaw issue. It made a big difference in my appearance (I had already had my lazy eye corrected in sixth grade). When I went back to school on the first day of my senior year, the first person that saw me didn't even recognize me. She walked right by me. When I said something to her, she just stood there staring at me. She remarked that I looked completely different, and she asked what I had done. I told her I had jaw surgery over the summer. She told me I looked pretty. I literally had no idea how to react. I had never been called pretty before. Other people complimented me too, but I couldn't receive their compliments. I felt unworthy of them. I still felt ugly, awkward, and rejected. My outside appearance had changed, but my inside was still dark, wounded, and hurting. I still had no self-confidence, no self-esteem, and continued to behave in ways that caused people to reject me. I couldn't stop acting that way, no matter how hard I tried. I wanted to understand my behavior, but I couldn't make sense of it. I believed deep down inside that this was just how I was wired. That was my personality, and it would never change. It affected every aspect of my life, relationships, career, everything.

I got a job right out of high school, but I wasn't able to move ahead or learn new things because I was too embarrassed to ask questions. I thought they would think I was stupid. The worst part was I knew I was bright; I knew I was capable, but I was paralyzed by the fear of failure. I was doing well in my current position, so I just stayed there, safe, too afraid to extend myself.

Eventually, I met my husband, fell in love, and became engaged. I couldn't understand what he saw in me. To me, I was awkward, nerdy, and unattractive. But he didn't see me that way. He was the first person to ever make me feel accepted for who I was. Early in our marriage, a family member encouraged us to give our hearts to Christ, and we began a relationship with Jesus. I immediately began to feel peace down deep inside. I knew something transformed on the inside, but on the outside, I was still behaving in ways that brought rejection and judgment. We attended church and learned more about God. I began to believe God could help me change the way I acted. I prayed and told Him I didn't want to be timid anymore, and I was tired of having no self-esteem. I wanted to be a different person.

One day at church, it was announced they were starting a twelve-week class called "Search for Significance." They explained it was a class for anyone dealing with issues that kept them from moving forward in life. I needed to sign up. With my husband's work schedule and two small children, I wasn't sure if I could commit to twelve weeks, but I was determined to try. God used that "Search for Significance" class to literally change my life. We studied fear of rejection, fear of failure, shame, and other mindsets that can prevent us from feeling good about ourselves. The week we talked about shame, I felt that God was impressing upon me that this was the mindset keeping me in those same patterns of behavior I desired to change. I thought to myself, *I'm not ashamed of anything. I don't understand.*

But God helped me see that all those years ago, all of the teasing about my looks had made me ashamed of who I was. It made me hate myself, inside and out. I had never even thought of that before. But suddenly it became crystal clear. I shared in class about what I felt God was revealing to me, and told them about being bullied. I thought they would all think I was a big crybaby.

Get over it.

It was twenty years ago.

I was embarrassed to tell them about it, and almost didn't, out of fear of what they would think. It was hard, but when I shared my story, they were very understanding. They made me realize it was okay that I felt hurt by the numerous situations I endured.

What happened next was amazing! This may sound weird to some of you, but I promise, it's all-true. Two days after I had shared my story, I was feeling very melancholy all day, like I was on the verge of crying any moment, but I didn't know why. That evening, as I was getting into my car to go somewhere, and pulled halfway down my driveway, the tears just started coming. I cried and cried, like I had never cried in my life. Gut-wrenching cries.

There I was, sitting in my car, in the middle of my driveway, crying my heart out. Yet all the while, I literally felt as if someone was standing in front of me, pulling a rope from my gut, out through my mouth. It was the strangest feeling, yet it felt wonderful. My head was filled with images from all those times I had been humiliated and made fun of. And as that rope was pulled, those images went with it. It was so weird! I knew in my heart that it was God, pulling out all the junk I buried down deep inside me for all those years. I sat there for over an hour. I eventually pulled myself together and went back inside. My husband clearly saw I had been crying, so I tried to explain what I experienced. It was hard to put into words.

I felt so light, so different.

So free.

It felt wonderful.

Over the next few days and weeks, I felt like an entirely different person. I didn't recognize myself. I was full of joy for the first time in my life. I was friendlier and more light-hearted. My husband said I didn't seem like the same person. I felt good about myself for the first time. I knew God removed all the old pain, and he healed every emotional wound I carried all those years. I went from feeling wounded to feeling whole.

The transformation didn't happen overnight. It took about a year for my personality to completely transform. I had to learn how to be a new me. My self-esteem was restored, and because of that, I became much more self-confident. I believed in myself for the first time in a long time. Friends and family would remark on the changes they saw in me.

That was twenty years ago, and I still marvel at what God did in my life. Since then, I have had a heart for hurting people. I want to see people restored to the person God designed them to be. I meet people sometimes, and I can tell they are emotionally wounded, and I want to tell them they don't have to stay in that place. I don't want anyone to go through life never knowing what it feels like to be whole, instead of broken. Our God is a God of restoration. He will bring beauty from ashes if we will allow Him to work in our lives.

I was bullied, but now I feel beloved, thanks to God's grace and love for me.

Elizabeth Broz is an aspiring writer who desires to introduce the healing power of Jesus to those who are living with emotional wounds. She resides with her husband in the Dallas, Texas area. You may contact Elizabeth at ebroz2016@gmail.com.

Thoughts to Ponder
from Bullied to Beloved

1. God sees you as His treasure.

2. God says vengeance is His.

3. Do not listen to what the world says about you. Listen to what God says about you.

**How do you think God sees you?
How do you see yourself?**

---

*You are the God who sees me, for she said,
"I have now seen the One who sees me."*
— Genesis 16:13

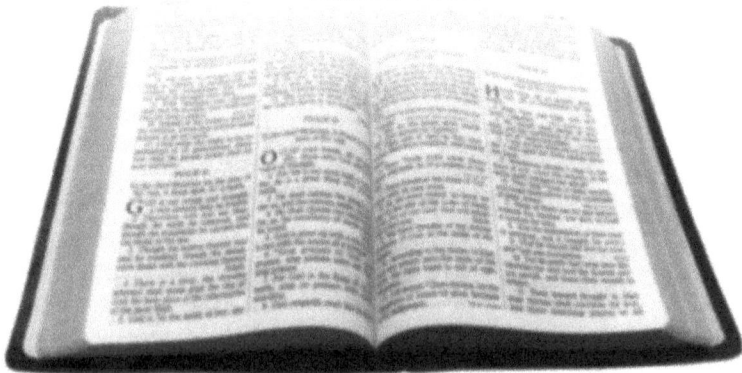

Feared Forgiveness
by Lisa Burkhardt Worley

Have you ever battled with fear? What do you think most people are afraid of?

Studies reveal over 40 percent of all people dread speaking in front of a group. 32 percent fear high places, then there is a whole slew of fears that follow: insects, financial problems, deep water, sickness and loneliness.

Growing up, I struggled with three different fears; the first two: snakes and horses.

My fear of snakes materialized in early childhood when I attended my cousins' swim meet in San Antonio, Texas. My athletic cousins were exceptional swimmers, so it was fun to cheer them on to their countless ribbons. One of them made it as far as the Olympic Trials in the Butterfly.

However, one day, while they were competing, we heard a ruckus going on behind the natatorium. The kids at the meet ran around to the back of the venue, and to our horror, we witnessed men chopping the heads off a bed of baby rattlesnakes. From that point on, I detested snakes, and avoided them at all cost.

Now to horses. The reason I fear horses is because my grandmother, who I nicknamed "Nonnie," used to repeatedly ask, "You're not riding horses are you?" Why would Nonnie ask such a bizarre question? Because she worried I'd suffer the same fate as my father if I ever ventured into the saddle.

My father was a doctor, but he also enjoyed playing competitive polo on the weekends. Every Sunday, my dad's team faced other polo teams from all over the country, and it was a high level of competition.

One Sunday in December, while my expectant mother, half-sister and other family members enjoyed the afternoon polo match, tragedy struck, as my father keeled over, suffering a massive heart attack while on his polo pony. He was dead before he arrived at the hospital, at the age of 39.

Two months later, I was born.

Neither my mother nor my fourteen-year-old half-sister, Lori, ever recovered from the trauma of that day. In the scurry and confusion, Lori was left alone at the polo field and had to undergo years of counseling to overcome the shock of losing her beloved dad.

After Lori moved back with her mother in Pennsylvania, my mother and I lived off and on with my grandparents until I was about eight, because she couldn't handle life after the traumatic day at the polo field. She was heavily medicated on anti-depressants, a chain smoker and for many years, a drinker.

When we weren't living with my grandparents, my life reminded me of the 1993 movie, *Ground Hog Day*. In that movie, actor Bill Murray portrays a weatherman on location doing a news story about the groundhog and his shadow. However, it's not just a one-day scenario. Mysteriously, every day Murray wakes up, it's Ground Hog Day all over again. Same hotel. Same television crew. Same assignment.

Every day I'd leave for school, my mother would be sitting in a chair, drinking and smoking a cigarette. I'd come home and find her in the same chair, drinking and smoking a cigarette, almost catatonic, and unable to engage with me.

I was a lonely child.

Have you ever been lonely?

I craved love.

Have you ever felt unloved? I can't remember my mother every hugging me. I was also embarrassed by my mother. I could not understand why she wasn't like other moms, and I didn't want friends to come play at my house.

Now I'll share my third fear.

I was afraid of ever being anything like my mother. It's a fear that drove me throughout childhood and the majority of my adult life.

Perhaps you have the same fear I had. Maybe you had a parent who was not the parent you longed for, and you are still trying to recover from it.

By the time I entered high school, my mom and I lived in a tiny one-bedroom apartment, and I spent as much time away from the apartment as I could. It was saturated with smoke and very depressing. I just wanted to get away. I was also headed down the wrong road, experimenting with alcohol by age thirteen.

But one day, my friend, Leslie, decided to take a bold risk. With five minutes left in our freshman English class, she asked if I wanted to accept Christ as my Lord and Savior. I said, "Why not?" What did I have to lose? I was looking for something new. Becoming a Christian had to be better than the life I was living, and the environment I was living in. So she explained to me that sin was separating me from God, and I needed to confess the things I had done wrong and believe in Jesus Christ to close the gap caused by my sin. I believed "For God so loved the world that He gave His one and only Son, so whoever believes in him shall not perish but have eternal life" (John 3:16).

So at that moment, I prayed with my friend, Leslie. I asked Jesus to come into my heart, and things did change for a while.

Instead of traveling down the wrong road in high school, I got involved in positive constructive activities. I exhibited hope and believed I had a future for the first time. My grades improved. My leadership tendencies surfaced as I founded a girls' Christian organization at school, because at the time, only boys could be members of the Fellowship of Christian Athletes. Frustrated with the lack of girls' sports at our high school, I also started the girls' basketball and volleyball teams at our school.

My friend Leslie didn't stop with leading me to Christ. She and her family took me to church every Sunday and between services, I spent the whole day at their house. I often sat at the feet of Leslie's mom, studying what a Godly woman looked like. I asked her a million questions and learned a lot about Jesus and His love during those years.

But discovering what a normal mom was like made mine seem much worse, so as soon as I graduated from high school, I was off to college, never planning to return home to my mother. I was a runner, running away from my greatest fear at top speed.

My mother worsened after I left. She tended to stray off the medication that regulated her, and the results weren't good. Often times, the local authorities were called in because she exhibited socially unacceptable behavior, and most times, she ended up at the state hospital. So my mother was the big secret I didn't talk about.

Meanwhile I slipped away from the faith. I call the seventeen years after high school, the lost years. I did not spend time in Bible study, sporadically went to church, and wasn't growing in my faith.

I pursued a career as a television sportscaster before women engaged in that type of profession. When I decided to be a sportscaster, the only females in the business were Miss Americas, so I thought it was time for a woman who played and understood sports to enter the field. Many people tried to talk me out of going down this career road, but I was determined and enjoyed a modicum of success in the business.

I landed my first real job in Chattanooga, Tennessee, where I worked three years before being hired at the CBS affiliate in my hometown of San Antonio. Now you ask, why would I go back home when I was running from my mother?

I still didn't have much to do with my mother when I returned. I think God wanted me to meet my husband, who I met six months after I returned to San Antonio.

I remained somewhat estranged from my mother and loved working in my hometown, but I had a dream of becoming an ESPN SportsCenter anchor, so I hired an agent to help me realize that dream. I finally received a big break when HBO Sports asked to interview me for a correspondent position on the show, "Inside the NFL." The only problem was, I was seven-and-a half months pregnant with our first son, Kyle. I needed to fly to New York City right away, before I was unable to travel anymore.

I remember that trip well. For the interview I wore a dark slimming dress so I wouldn't look too pregnant, and I also remember taking my shoes off on the plane and not being able to wear them when I landed because my feet were so swollen. I also thought, *I don't know how they're going to get past this big belly of mine.* But the interview went well. The HBO Executive Producer's wife had recently given birth to twins, so he understood my oversized body was temporary, and I landed the job. Eight weeks after I gave birth to our 8 lb., 13 oz. baby boy, I was off to Salem, Oregon to do my first HBO story about the Oregon NFL Lottery.

For a year, I kept my job in San Antonio and flew all over the country covering football stories about the NFL. The following year, I had another huge job opportunity to be an anchor and reporter for the Madison Square Garden Network, hosting a show called the MSG Sports Desk. In television, New York City is the top market in the country, so landing this job would mean I made it to the top of my field. It was a great opportunity, and I also thought it was a potential stepping-stone to ESPN.

My husband agreed to follow me to New York City, so I accepted the job, and this Texas girl loved the Big Apple! We lived in New Rochelle, New York and to get to work, I'd catch a cab to the train station, then rode the Metro North train for thirty minutes to Grand Central Station, hopped a subway to Times Square, then grabbed a different subway train to Penn Station. Once at Penn Station, I'd walk up the stairs to Madison Square Garden, and traveled up a number of ramps to my office.

It was especially interesting when the Barnum and Bailey Circus camped at Madison Square Garden for a couple of weeks. I'd head up the ramp to my office, and it was not unusual to see a trainer bathing an elephant on the ramp. It was always a great adventure.

A year before my contract was up, I received a call from the President of ESPN. He wanted to have lunch and talk, so we did, and he expressed an interest in hiring me after my contract expired at MSG. He was throwing around details like a five-year-deal to anchor SportsCenter. He said ESPN hadn't hired me before because they didn't know what I could do, but now that they were seeing me on a regular basis, things changed. So I thought I was close to a dream realized.

But a year later, when my contract was almost up at MSG, the bottom dropped out. In the same week, I was not renewed on either the HBO or the MSG contract. HBO was the biggest surprise. I received a call from the Executive Producer of HBO Sports, the same guy who hired me. He phoned from the Wimbledon tennis tournament because HBO had television rights at the time. He said, "We weren't looking to replace you. We know what kind of work you did, but Mrs. _____ (I won't say the name) wants to do it." She was already on a major network, and married to the CBS Morning News anchor, so she was higher profile talent than I was.

I was in shock and hurt by HBO, even though I knew it was just business. I went from six figures to zero overnight.

Have you ever had a financial crash like that? Have you or your spouse ever been laid off from work?

We were overwhelmed with fear and panic because we could no longer afford our home in expensive Westchester County. My husband informed me that we needed to move to Connecticut.

"No! Not that!"

I loved New York. I enjoyed the environment, the Broadway shows, the shopping. I was like Eva Gabor in the old program, Green Acres, who said, "New York is where I'd rather stay. I get allergic smelling hay. I just adore a penthouse view; darling, I love you, but just give me Park Avenue."

I was also mad at God. After a seventeen-year estrangement, I reconnected by asking Him in anger, "Why did you do this to me?" "Why would You take away my livelihood?"

God didn't answer my questions immediately. I lost my protest to remain in New York, so we packed up and moved to Connecticut.

During this time, we also searched for a church.

It often takes life turning upside down before we finally look up.

I closed my eyes and randomly pointed to a church in the Yellow Pages, and we tried it out. From the moment we walked in the door, I knew it was the church where God wanted us. A woman immediately reached out to us, introduced me to other women my age, and directed me to a Bible study for young mothers, held weekly. I thought, *I'd like to try that.* So I joined a group of moms, many of them seekers like myself, and studied the Bible for the first time. It was interesting that the study was on love. It's what God knew I still needed. Love. His love.

After delving into the Word and praying regularly for about six months, God finally came back to the questions I asked, with attitude, when the bottom fell out of my life.

"Why did you take my career away?"

"Why did you take my livelihood away?"

He said, "Lisa, I gave you an incredible national platform to glorify Me and you didn't do it. I had to take it away to get your attention."

I was devastated and remorseful. The past seventeen years, full of sinful behavior, flashed before my eyes. With tears rolling down my cheeks, I promised God, "If You give me another opportunity, I will not only give my career to You, I'll give You my life." That day, I surrendered all to my Maker.

Not surprising, about a week later, ESPN called my agent, asking if I'd be interested in doing some free-lance reporting for them. My dream resurfaced, and I didn't think twice about accepting the job.

I reported for ESPN for about six months when I received an offer to return to San Antonio to resume my old anchoring job at the CBS Affiliate. This time God was at the center of my life and my decisions, so I prayed about a job change for the first time ever. Out of His love for me, the Lord provided a taste of reporting at ESPN, and I knew it was not a life conducive to being a mom or a wife. Full-time reporters were sometimes away from home for weeks, traveling from story-to-story-to-story, and I knew that would not work for our family.

The only way I could remain at ESPN would be if they offered me a SportsCenter anchor position, my dream.

Otherwise, I would return to San Antonio. Deep down, I knew I could make more of an impact for the Lord as a big fish in a smaller pond than a small fish in a very big pond.

Not surprising, all ESPN could offer was a full-time reporting job, so I was probably the first and last person in ESPN history to turn down a national television position with the well-respected sports network.

A long-term stint at ESPN wasn't part of God's plan, and I was okay with it. The desires of my heart morphed into what God desired for me.

Are you willing to relinquish your dream for God's plan?

So I returned home again, and God's first assignment wasn't about slipping back into my old sports anchoring shoes.

While that happened, it wasn't the main thing.

God asked me to honor my mother, for the first time in my life.

It was time to quit running. I had been running away for a long time. I needed to face my greatest fear, my mother, and honor her despite all those troubled childhood years. By that time, she was living in a group home because she couldn't handle life on her own. Honoring my mother meant visiting her regularly, taking my son to see her, and providing for her material needs.

It was amazing how Jesus worked in my life.

At some point during this period of time, I also forgave my mother. Through a Bible study, I realized how much of my sin God forgave; so I thought, *If God can forgive me for all the wrong I did in my life, who am I not to forgive my mother?*

I had reconnected with my mother for about two years when my mom called and said she needed a pair of shoes. I was anxious to buy the pair of shoes for her. I wanted her to have new shoes more than anything. (That's how far I'd come.) At lunch that day, I ran to a local department store and tried to find the perfect pair. I didn't know why at the time, but I was in a hurry to buy the shoes. I realized later God was letting me know time was short, because before I could run the shoes over to my mother, I received a call from her caregiver. She told me my mom suffered a massive heart attack, and was rushed to the hospital, where she lay in a coma.

I spent the last week of my mother's life at her side, stroking her hair and telling her I loved her. After she died, I know I heard the Lord say, "Now you understand what my unconditional love is like." I made sure my mom wore her new shoes when she was laid to rest.

One of my favorite Bible verses is: "I will repay you for the years the locusts have eaten" (Joel 2:25).

Have you had a lot of locusts eating at your life over the years?

There were numerous locusts gnawing at me for years, but God restored my life. He was also able to do a much greater work in and through me once I forgave my mother, and I was no longer afraid.

In the late 90's, God revealed it was time to leave television. I argued with him again. I was growing by leaps and bounds in my faith and using the television platform to glorify Him, speaking about Him whenever I was asked. But I didn't argue long. I trusted He knew why He wanted me out of the business.

And it became very clear. As a television sports anchor, I couldn't commit to regular ministry work. I could only teach Sunday school on Sunday morning because that was the only time I knew I had off. Otherwise, I worked nights and weekends covering sporting events. It was a very inconsistent schedule.

I scanned the want ads for the first time ever and landed a job as the Public Relations Manager at San Antonio

International Airport. Because I had a day job, God was able to use me far more, and I had additional quality time with my husband and two boys.

In 2003, the Lord called me into full-time ministry and seminary. I think I was the only one in seminary aspiring to be an author and Christian inspirational speaker.

And God directed me to minister to women. I had worked all my life in male dominated professions. It's just like God to call us to something out of left field that we would have never chosen on our own. He gave me the ministry's name, Pearls of Promise, to help women overcome past dysfunction. You may know a pearl is formed through irritation in an oyster shell. In the same way, God can make something beautiful out of the irritations in our lives, if we let Him.

He did it for me, a poor fatherless child. He raised my life out of the pit and set me on the right path. He created beautiful pearls out of the hardships and I am forever grateful.

Yes, the television life was very exciting, but I relate to what the Bible says in Philippians 3:8: "What is more, I consider everything a loss because of the surpassing worth of knowing Christ Jesus my Lord, for whose sake I have lost all things. I consider them garbage, that I may gain Christ."

I'd give up the television career today if it meant not knowing Christ.

Would you give up your career, with all the accolades, if it meant not having a relationship with Christ?

Because, with Jesus in my life, I feel loved again. I am no longer lonely. I am not embarrassed when I'm in the midst of trials. Instead of running away from problems, I run straight to my Father's arms. I am no longer afraid.

Lisa Burkhardt Worley is an award-winning author of three books, speaker, blogger, and international radio show host. She is the founder of Pearls of Promise Ministries, and is the Director of Special Projects for Roaring Lambs Ministries. You can find Lisa at: www.pearlsofpromiseministries.com.

Thoughts to Ponder
from Feared Forgiveness

1. God has a well thought out plan for your life.

2. God is bigger than our fears.

3. God will always woo us back to intimacy with Him.

**What fears do you need to confront?
Who do you need to forgive?**

*I sought the LORD, and he answered me;
he delivered me from all my fears.* — Psalm 34:4

Masters in Messes
by Pat McNatt

I am a nurse, and sometimes we nurses have to do some unpleasant things. I've worked in several different specialties, all the way from the top of your head to the bottom of your feet, and several places in between. I've been in the medical field for forty years, but for the past ten years, I've been employed as a pediatric GI nurse. Therefore, we do endoscopies and colonoscopies every day. I definitely earned my master's degree in messes when it comes to my profession, but I also earned a Master of Messes when it comes to life.

When I was in high school, I had a lot of friends who were boys, but I didn't have any "boyfriends." While my friends were all dating, I sat at home. So I made the statement I was going to marry the first person that asked me, because I was afraid no one else would propose. That is exactly what I did. I graduated in May, and married in June. I asked Jesus into my heart when I was ten, but hadn't experienced any spiritual growth, so I didn't realize I was supposed to pray about whom I was going to marry. That is when I enrolled in my first course to earn my Master of Messes.

I wanted either two or four children. God gave me four, but he only intended for me to raise three. I adopted my first child, a three-month-old little boy, when I was twenty-one. If you think hard, you can probably guess what happened next. Yes, the next year I gave birth to another little baby boy.

However, that was the one God did not intend for me to raise. The doctor came into my room at midnight and said he wasn't sure the baby was going to make it. Of course, I was crying and praying all night long. The next morning the doctor returned and asked if I wanted to go to the nursery with him. Of course, I said yes. I waited outside the nursery while he went inside, examined him, and pronounced him dead. That was the first time in my life I felt like my heart shattered into a million pieces and would never be the same. Little did I know there would be many more instances in the future.

Three years later, we lived on the island of Guam. I sent letters out to several different medical facilities regarding the adoption of another child. I got one response. There was a little two-year-old girl in Thailand available for adoption. Within a matter of a few months, we completed the process. I was happy for a short time. I had a boy and girl. What more could I ask for? However, it wasn't long before I started having that deep longing desire to have another baby. Three years later, God blessed me with a healthy baby girl. It took ten years to conceive this little bundle of joy.

As you can see, having a family wasn't easy for me, but it was a piece of cake compared to raising them. There weren't any traumatic experiences until they started school. That is when I enrolled in my second course toward my Master of Messes.

My son had low self-esteem from the beginning. He struggled at everything he did. When I went to my first parent teacher conference, I knew they were going to tell me, besides being cute and adorable, he was also extremely intelligent. I was disappointed when all my son's teacher said was that he spent a lot of time in the hall. Once he got into junior high, things became very difficult. He was on drugs long before I knew anything about it. Then he started running away from home. We tried public schools, private school, counseling and rehab several times. Each time he would promise us the moon, but he was never able to follow through.

One night I was crying myself to sleep, as I often did, and I was having a one-sided conversation with God. I told him not to put anything else on me, because I couldn't take anymore. I eventually went to sleep, but received a phone call at two in the morning. It was a hospital in Colorado asking for permission to treat my son because he overdosed on drugs. One of the first thoughts I had was, *I guess God will tell me when I have had enough and when I haven't.* He was in Colorado, and we lived in Oklahoma. How he got to Colorado, I will never know.

The last semester of his senior year I received a call from the school saying he walked out of class again. They were done with him. He left home to be on his own and continued his unhealthy lifestyle.

My oldest daughter was two when we adopted her. She was cute and jabbered all the time, but could not speak a word of English. I could tell her to do something and she would just look at me. Her brother would say, "Momma said..." and tell her what I said. Funny, she understood everything he told her. The amusing part is when she started speaking English, she began every sentence with "Momma said..." because that is what her big brother did.

She never had any problem with self-esteem. She was confident and did well in school until the sixth grade. It was at that time she tried to tell me her dad sexually abused her. The two of them were like oil and water. In my mind, I thought she was trying to get him into trouble, or perhaps she wanted some of the attention her brother was getting. Besides, that is what happens in *other* families, right? It was never mentioned again.

Once my daughter entered junior high, she thought school was a great place to go and socialize, but she had no desire to go to class. Her brother was in high school at the time, and I was getting several calls every week regarding one of them. She insisted if she went to a private school she would do better. We enrolled her in a private school and before the semester was up, history repeated itself. She ran away once, and the police picked her up a week later. After she got into high school she left home again, and eventually moved to California.

We all know it is during the difficult times in our life that we grow spiritually. Trust me, I was doing a lot of growing. I was attending ladies Bible studies, going to conferences and retreats. I turned to the fourth chapter of Philippians, often because it is known as the joy chapter. I would read it over and over. I can't tell you how many times I have quoted, "I can do all things through Christ who strengthens me" (Philippians 4:13 NKJ).

The only steady job my husband had was seven years in the Air Force. The rest of the time I was the primary provider for the family. We didn't have a good home life. He was hard on the kids, and life was very stressful. I realized I was severely depressed. After coming home from work, I would cry or sleep all evening. After twenty-three years of marriage, I filed for divorce. It was at that time I found out my husband committed adultery numerous times, and I was convinced what my daughter told me years earlier about being abused was true. That is something I will have to live with forever.

Now I have graduated, with honors.

I spent twenty-three years in a bad marriage, my son ruined his life with drugs, and my ex-husband abused my oldest daughter. I also filed bankruptcy. I felt like such a failure. That was the lowest point in my life. I knew God was in control, but I struggled. I couldn't find where I belonged. I didn't want to go to a ladies' Bible study, and I didn't feel like I fit in a couples' class.

A few months later, our Minister to College Students asked me to work in the college ministry. I was very hesitant; after all, I didn't have a very good track record with teenagers. He encouraged me to give it a try. The next Sunday I went to their Sunday school class and I loved it. They were full of life and energy. They didn't care I was by myself, because they were by themselves, too. Before long, I started going to their Wednesday night Bible study, which consisted of about 200 students who met at ten p.m. on the Oklahoma University campus. That is when the healing began!

God showed me he still had a purpose and plan for my life. Joel 2:25 says, "I will repay you for the years the locusts have eaten." I found myself leading girls' Bible studies, going on mission trips, and attending conferences. I was able to do things I had never done as a young person because I married so young. However, after seven years I felt like God was telling me my time was up there, and he had something else for me. I didn't know where I was going to live, where I would be working, or where I would be going to church. But, I didn't have an ounce of fear. God did so many amazing things in my life I couldn't wait to see what was next. He provided everything I needed, when I needed it.

At the suggestion of my pastor, I attended a different church with a large adult singles ministry. It was there I met my second husband, and we married later that year. When we tied the knot, he was working for Mardel's. The following year he took a job with LifeWay, and we moved to Texas. He managed the LifeWay store in Plano for seven years; then they closed it. We were shocked. Because of his age, he had a very difficult time finding a job, and we were not prepared for him to retire. A friend suggested we open our own store. He had been in retail all his life; opening stores for other companies, and had been in Christian retail for twelve years.

We prayed about it, and felt like that is what God wanted us to do. We spent nearly every dime we had, and opened Abundant Life Christian store in McKinney.

It was beautiful. On the front door was the verse in John that says, "I came that they may have life and have it abundantly" (John 10:10 ESV). Over the Bibles was the verse in Isaiah: "The grass withers, the flowers fade, but the word of God will stand forever" (Isaiah 40:8 ESV). Over the Bible studies was Ephesians 3:20: "He is able to do immeasurably more than all we ask or imagine." We were so proud of it.

The first year wasn't bad. But, by the end of the second year it was evident, due to the economy and construction, we needed to close the store. To say I prayed about the store is an understatement. I cried, begged, and pleaded with God for our store to be successful. I knew if God wanted our store to be successful it would be successful.

He is bigger than all those things. And, for some reason God said no. I found myself filing for bankruptcy for the second time in my life. The first time I was angry. This time I was sad. God hurt my feelings. We were doing our best, and our best wasn't good enough. I will admit it took me a long time to get over this. But God was patient with me. I finally realized I don't have to like or understand everything God does, but I do have to accept it. After all, I know he makes no mistakes.

A couple of years later, I received a call on a Thursday night from my oldest daughter. She and her brother were both living in Nevada. She called to tell me my son, who I hadn't seen in seven years, was in the hospital again and they didn't think he would make it through the weekend. I said, "You tell him mom is coming" and she did just that. I was able to get a direct flight early the next morning. I didn't have a clue what I would find when I got there. When she picked me up at the airport, she told me he was sitting up in the bed talking, but the doctor expected him to go downhill after I arrived.

We spent the whole day together talking about everything. He reassured me of his salvation and told me what his wishes were. That evening I went to dinner with my daughter and then on to my hotel room. He called me at ten p.m. and said, "I just called to say I love you." I said, "I love you too, and I will see you in the morning."

I arrived the next morning to find out he crashed during the night and they intubated him. That is the one thing he did not want. As a matter of fact, he would look at me and motion to take it out. I signed the papers and had it removed. He rallied for a short time. Every once in a while he would sit straight up and say, "Mom." I would hold and comfort him until he fell back asleep. He eventually went into a deep coma and never woke up again. Several hours later he took his last breath. My son ruined his health with drugs, and due to his lifestyle, he never came home.

We expect to someday sit beside a parent and say goodbye. We know there is a fifty-fifty chance we will have to say goodbye to our spouse. However, we never entertain the idea of sitting at the bedside of one of our children and saying goodbye to them. I am thankful God allowed us to have that final time together on this side of heaven, so we'd have closure. He allowed me to hold my son and sing to him. I was able to look him in the face and tell him I loved him. For that I will always be grateful.

Often times, there is good that comes out of bad. My son's death resurrected my relationship with my oldest daughter. I have now lost two children I don't want to lose another. My daughter never came home either because of her lifestyle. Twenty years prior to this time she called me from California to tell me she was gay. That put a strain on our relationship, because I didn't know how to deal with it.

A couple of years ago I went through Stephen Ministries training. The one phrase I heard over and over was, "It is not about you." I finally got it. I realized the reason I was having such a hard time accepting my daughter's lifestyle is because I was making it all about me; my pride, my self-esteem, my failure as a parent. It was like a huge weight taken off my shoulders. I now had the ability to love her the way I should have all along. She hasn't changed, but God has changed me.

In spite of the difficult times in my life, I am blessed beyond measure. If God was going to give me one child that was easy to raise, I am glad he saved her until last because I was tired. She graduated from high school with honors. She married after her first year of college but, in spite of being married and working, she graduated in four years with honors. Her goal was to pass her CPA exam, buy a house, and then have a baby. She did just that.

She and my son-in-law have given me two beautiful grandchildren who live a couple of miles from us. I have been a large part of their lives since they were babies, and God has taught me so much through them. They truly are the light of my life. I feel like I have been given a second chance with a family.

I am doing things with my grandchildren I never did with my own children, because I was so busy making a living and doing what I thought were the important things.

I know all grandchildren are special, but let me tell you why these two are extra special. I have a grandson from my oldest daughter I will never know, and two granddaughters from my son I will never know. Therefore, I absolutely cherish every moment I have with my two beautiful grandchildren.

You see, being a Christian doesn't mean life is going to be easy. What is does mean is that we have someone who loves us unconditionally, and we can call on Him twenty-four hours a day. He knows our heartaches and sees every tear that we shed. Nothing catches him by surprise and he will meet our every need. The common thread throughout my testimony is God's provision. He always provided everything I needed spiritually, physically, emotionally, and financially. I may have a Master of Messes, but God, through his grace, also awarded me a Doctorate in Restoration, even though I did not deserve it.

Pat McNatt is a speaker and author of "From Restoration ... to Rejoicing." She leads Women's Ministry at her home church, and serves as a Roaring Lambs Testimony Workshop Facilitator. To schedule her to speak at your next ladies event or to schedule a Testimony Workshop, go to pat@patmcnatt.com.

Thoughts to Ponder
from Master of Messes

1. Life is messy.

2. When we are obedient to Him, God can help clean up our messes.

3. Life's challenges provide God's curriculum.

How has God worked good out of one of your messes?

And we know that in all things God works for the good of those who love him, who have been called according to his purpose. — Romans 8:28

Blinded and Upside Down

by Sheila Garza Figueroa

Have you ever seen the commercial on television showing a woman at her back door, asking an animal, who she thinks is a cat, but it's not, "Do you want to come in and snuggles with mama?" Then you see a raccoon walk in; and later the spot shows the woman in bed with the raccoon, stretched out at her feet, and she says, "Good kitty." The woman thinks everything and everyone is okay, right? She thinks she sees clearly, right? But she really doesn't because her vision is not one hundred percent. Well, that was me! Have you ever thought you were thinking and seeing pretty clearly, and you really weren't?

Throughout my high school and college years I did not attend church; nor did I read my Bible on a regular basis. *Okay, be truthful Sheila.* I read the Bible at Easter and Christmas. I prayed to God when I needed good grades or help during a crisis. That was it. I never prayed consistently. My parents did not attend church so I did not make it a priority in my life. I always believed God is God and that Jesus is his Son. I have always believed there is a Holy Spirit and the three are one. I just never had a relationship with God.

Fast forward to my early adult years.

During those years I was a perfectionist, usually stressed and worried. Needless to say, I didn't have a whole lot of fun. I thought I could do it all and was frustrated many times when things didn't go as planned. I was an organizer, and I always wanted things to be perfect. I carried this fear inside of me that people would find out I wasn't perfect. Some of my friends would tell me about Jesus Christ, having a relationship with Him, and invite me to their church, but I always had an excuse. I was busy living life, planning life, and did not have time for God, much less attend a church service.

Yet, there was something always missing in my life, even though I was busy. No matter how preoccupied I was, there was never what I call fulfillment or peace. I always had to do more and more, regardless if I could see ahead or not. Make a goal, reach a goal; it never was enough.

I finally gave in to one of my friends, or so I thought I was giving in, to attend a church service back in the late 1980's. The words the pastor spoke that day reached deep into my heart. I started crying. I thought something was wrong with me. My girlfriend stepped out because she was coughing a lot. Why would I cry in front of a bunch of strangers? They didn't know me. They wouldn't even want to get to know me. If they did, they would find out I was not perfect. I learned that "all have sinned and fall short of the glory of God" (Romans 3:23). At the end of the service, I asked Jesus into my life. I prayed for Jesus to forgive all the bad and the not so good things I had done and asked forgiveness for all the unkind words I said to people.

Have you ever thought, *Well, it wasn't that bad?* It really was. The thoughts that went through my head were especially bad. Some of them would make your toes curl for sure. Do toes really curl? Hmmmm... That's a question for another day. I learned Scripture says, "For Christ also suffered once for sins, the righteous for the unrighteous, that he might bring us to God, being put to death in the flesh but made alive in the spirit" (1 Peter 3:18 ESV).

After I prayed to become a Christian, I began to see subtle changes in my life. I wasn't as bent on being perfect every single day.

Woohoo! Thank God for that one.

I need to add here that I never had an "aha" moment or a "mountain top experience" as some people call it. When people shared the Lord spoke to them and told them whatever, I remember smiling and going "uh huh" and thinking, *These people are out of their minds. God doesn't speak to anyone. Not really.*

However, I began to see I needed God and his son Jesus more and more. My blurry spiritual vision improved. Cobwebs came off of my eyes, slowly but surely. I was changing. There are verses in the Bible that speak about this. "Therefore, if anyone is in Christ, he is a new creation; the old has passed away; behold, the new has come. All this is from God, who through Christ reconciled us to himself and gave us the ministry of reconciliation" (2 Corinthians 5:17–18).

Just when I thought I was spiritually mature, I endured a trial that literally knocked me flat. In September 2009, the retina in my left eye spontaneously detached. All you need to know about this is I don't want any of you to have to go through it, okay? To date, I have had seven surgeries to reattach my retina. After the first two surgeries in September and October of 2009, I was quarantined at home for a month, which means I was not allowed out of the house, not outside on the porch, not outside to get the mail.

Nothing.

I stayed on my stomach for 45 minutes out of every 60 minutes, 24 hours a day. Do you know how hard that was? The person who was busy, but getting much better at not being too busy? I would be a liar if I told you I thanked God every single day while I was on my stomach, but I did remember to thank Him that there were retinal surgeons, trained in this kind of procedure. I thanked God that it was 2009, and not fifteen years before when there were no medical procedures to fix a retinal detachment.

So, this "eye situation," as I like to call it, forced me to either hear Scripture from the pastors on television or hear Scriptures being read on an audio CD. As I began to hear the words in the Bible, and I do mean hear with a capital H, more things began to change for me. I was more aware. I could actually "feel" God's presence. I was more alive; and even though my left eye was covered, I began to see even more clearly.

During these times people brought over food, groceries, telephoned me, and sent me wonderful cards and notes. People prayed for me, and still are, because my vision has not fully returned. I do thank God for all of them! I felt so much love and peace during that time.

Then on March 3, 2010, which happened to be my dear husband Raymond's birthday, I had a follow up appointment with the surgeon. I remember telling my Pastor I would call him after that appointment to give him the update on my situation. The update was not good. The surgeon told me that a part of my retina was folded. No! You want your eye doctor to tell you that you have a flat retina. Like the stomach, flat is good. The doctor said he was going to cryo it, which means freeze it, there in the office and put in a gas bubble to try to flatten out the retina. He was not hopeful it would work. If this didn't do the job, we would have to go in for another surgery.

Now keep in mind, up to this time, I had not broken down emotionally. Not really. Not a crying jag, not a "what the heck is going on" kind of conversation with the Lord. On the drive home, I started crying just a little. Raymond asked me, "Are you all right?" And I said, "Yes, I will be in a minute." Well, no not really.

When we came home, I lost it. I sat on the couch and cried and cried, and the tears made my eye hurt even more because it was frozen and it had a big patch of gauze on it. I could feel the tears stinging.

After I finished crying, my cell phone rang (another one of God's perfect timings) and my pastor said, "Sheila you didn't call me. What's happening?" I answered, "I didn't call you because I was having a fit." Without skipping a beat, he asked me "Was it a little fit or a big fit?" I told him "a big fit," with cuss words in my thoughts and everything, a crying jag." He said, "Sheila, big fits are good. God knows what you are going through. God knows what you feel. We are all praying for you." I said, "Thanks," and then told him what the doctor said.

There is a happy ending, the cryo ended up working and my retina is flat. Praise God for healing!

So, after giving you all this information, I have some things to tell you I learned while on my stomach for 45 minutes out of every hour.

Being a Christian does not guarantee you a life without bumps in the road. I gave my life to Jesus so that He can do with it what He wants. But I now have hope, and I have peace; and that is a beautiful thing.

Really good people, almost angel-like, do exist.

Some of them, I have learned, have really cool cell phones that have games on them. The games kept my husband's mind occupied while I was in surgery.

Some of them have loud laughs, kind eyes and kind words, are funny and have the patience of saints.

Some of them have an absolute love for chocolate chip cookies.

Some of them loan you the best books on tape.

Some of them can be intense, but they are oh, so sincere.

One friend actually laid on my living room floor, underneath my head so she could see me while we talked.

One friend bought and gave me my very first large print Bible.

There are many people who you never see but just know they are there.

God reminded me that my husband is truly my human rock and support.

I was shown that some of my friends love to cook and pray; they would do whatever I asked of them.

Kindness is a powerful thing.

It became clear to me God is real. I was reminded that God does love me. God used this forced quiet time to show me things about myself that were not pretty. He showed me that committees and other activities do go on without me, and that I don't have to say, "yes" to everything I am asked to do. I am only to trust and depend on Him. I desire to know Him and follow His principles. Why is that so hard at times? Well, I am human. I was reminded God is in control, not me. I also learned situations are never as bad as they seem.

I thank God that I never once dwelled on the thought that I would be blind in my left eye. My right eye, by the way, is 20/20 with my glasses. I thank God I am a Texan because in Texas it is legal to drive a car with one eye. I thank God I still have vision in my left eye. It is real blurry at the moment, but I have it. Some people have none. God's timing is perfect. We don't get that because we are not perfect. For some of us, that statement kills us. It used to kill me.

I learned good does come out of something not so good. It may be just a lesson for me to learn, or something that I can use to help others. I learned what praying really means. It means talking to God in my voice, with my words that I use every day.

It became clear to me if you don't feel God or think God is there, just believe He is because He is.

You are not abandoned. It is just not your moment in time to feel His presence. I learned that it is when our life is falling apart that our faith is tested. I believe I have true faith because I have more patience with life's obstacles now.

I was reminded I serve a living God, a resurrected God! Scripture says, "God is our refuge and strength, a very present help in trouble" (Psalm 46:1).

I learned that being in a growing relationship with Christ demands changes. Along with growth, this relationship challenges us to see possibilities for ourselves and a world that we had never imagined. God didn't save me to make life easy. He saved me to be in a relationship with Him, and what an exciting possibility that is for me today.

I am humbled by Jesus' concern for everyone and everything. With my busy and over-commitment, I forgot how Jesus really does love us and is concerned for our well-being. I have learned to not let the circumstances get *in* me; keep them around me, yes, but not get *in* me. I have learned that no matter how difficult our circumstances are, we can make it through anything this world tosses at us with the power of Christ running through us. God *is* my strength.

Reading the Bible (or hearing the words in the Bible) helps me to know the heart and will of God. God has given each one of us some area of giftedness in our lives and we need to use those gifts while discovering our purpose in life. I always said that if eating were a spiritual gift, I would be the most spiritual woman in the world. Ha!

I want to see my life as one that is obedient to the Lord.

God is faithful always.

God keeps his promises always.

Don't look at the storms around you, look at Jesus. Don't listen to your fears; trust God's promise to be with you. Don't succumb to your own troubled emotions; let the Holy Spirit take over.

I was so busy with various activities, including (gasp), church activities, that there was little time left for God. I learned I need to make a conscious decision, and then it takes action. I just can't talk about it; I have to do something. God gave me His son Jesus. He loves me that much. He forgave my sins. All of them, good, bad, and ugly. It is important to remember the times when God seemed especially close and to remember the difficult times God has brought me through, for it is a means of encouragement when things happen in our lives. God has brought me through many storms, and I thank him for that.

My goal now is to know Christ and to be obedient. It takes a lot of energy to fight Him and His plan for my life. So I'd rather use energy to know Him with everything I have.

I was a sinner, and I still am a sinner. I am not perfect. But I know God has forgiven me and loves me, and I will spend the rest of my life loving and serving Him. When I accepted Jesus Christ as Lord and Savior, I was sure of the forgiveness of sins, new life in Christ, and eternity in heaven.

I was blind, but now I see. "So clearly" means more than the difference between a raccoon and a cat. "So clearly" means more to me than you will ever know.

Sheila Figueroa was born and raised in San Antonio, Texas and has been married for 32 years to Raymond, a retired animal trainer at the San Antonio Zoo. She is a legal secretary and her hobbies include traveling around Texas, reading, cooking, and baking. Her email address is: shefig@earthlink.net.

Thoughts to Ponder

from Blinded and Upside Down

1. Sometimes God forces us to be still to hear His voice.

2. The world says, "Seeing is Believing." God says, "Believing is Seeing."

3. God uses His people to comfort others.

What has God said to you lately?

My eyes are ever on the Lord, for only he will release my feet from the snare. — Psalm 25:15

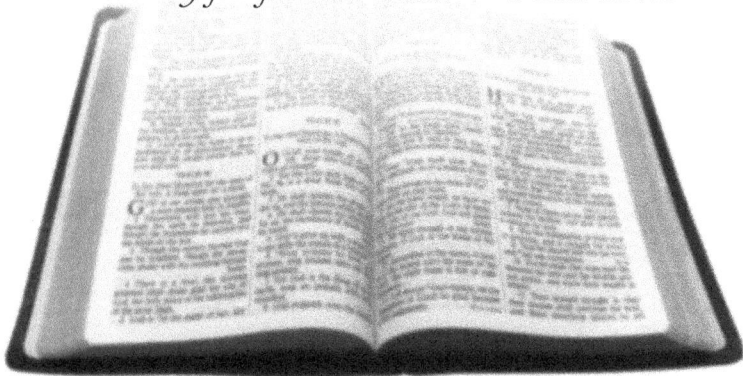

Guilty, but Not Charged
by Amy Hayes

Guilty!

The judged pronounced as the gavel came down hard. There I stood, head down, hands cuffed, ready to be carted away to my sentence—death! It all seemed like a dream. A dream, a dream, that's it! I awoke with a jolt, breathing hard and visibly shaken. Wow, what relief. Yet it all seemed so real, so possible. I shuddered as I shook off the disturbing dream.

But the truth was I lived every day of my life feeling guilty, as if somehow I was less than everyone else, unworthy of anything, including the air I breathed freely into my lungs. I was living life like an imposter. Feeling that if anyone knew the real me, they would laugh or even scoff. *What a joke*, I heard them thinking.

My parents were good people who took me to church, sent me to private school and tried to teach me to do what was right. I wanted to be good, to do right and make my parents proud. But regardless of how good I was, I never felt good about myself. The standards were always a little higher, never quite attainable. My worth was tied to how well I could perform. Approval and affirmation were non-existent. I lived in an emotional vacuum devoid of any love or affection.

School was one place I could shine. I always got really good grades, straight A's until tenth grade when I brought home that first B. I'll never forget the feeling of anxiety, knowing I'd failed. I nervously stood by while my dad, the perfectionist, scrupulously inspected my report card. He finally looked up over the rim of his glasses and said, "What happened here?" pointing to the 'B." My heart sank, as I felt that all too familiar feeling of "Not quite good enough."

I also excelled musically. At age thirteen, I ranked in the state as a pianist and was invited to play for the all-state competition. At fourteen, I sang the lead in my high school musical. I loved to sing, but I was painfully insecure. My dad was a singer, known in our community for his talent. He gave me a handful of lessons, but I was sure my vocal ability didn't impress him. He never commented on my performance, so I assumed the worst. I enjoyed the thrill of performing very much, but I kept it to myself, thinking my parents would not approve. I kept my emotions to myself with no one to share my joy. I lived a solitary existence inside my soul.

I continued to try and please my parents, following the rules, doing the best I could at all my endeavors. My parents never showed love nor said I love you. I longed to feel important, valuable and just plain loved. But all I felt was empty and hollow inside.

Eventually the luster of "being good" started to wear off. There didn't really seem to be anything in it for me, so I began to push the envelope a bit. I sought the attention of boys in an attempt to feel loved. I went on dates behind my parents' back, sneaking out after they were in bed. This secret life of deceit brought with it feelings of guilt and shame. I justified my actions in my mind thinking, "Would God really mind? All I wanted was a little love. Surely He understood."

As my high school graduation neared, I was filled with feelings of worthlessness and failure. Although I ranked second in my highly competitive class, the outward accolades did little to fill the void in my soul. I was looking for love and affirmation so I married my boyfriend shortly after graduation. I was two months pregnant at the wedding, but no one knew.

Shortly after the birth of our first child, my husband lost interest in me as my attention focused more and more on our daughter. Two more children arrived within seven years. I gained a bit of satisfaction from being a mom, but my husband's waning interest left me, once again, with feelings of failure and rejection.

I continued going to church trying to find the peace and comfort I desired, but the loneliness only continued to grow. My heart yearned to be cherished and men continued to be a snare. After ten painful years of marriage, I found myself in a full-blown affair.

The divorce was long and messy and involved a nasty custody battle. The children that had been the joy of my life were snatched from my hands. I was devastated, feeling as if my heart was ripped out of my chest. The rocky foundation of my life finally crumbled. I became pregnant by my lover who was in no way fit to be a husband and father. He was a drug addict.

My family and my church frowned upon divorce. In addition, my pastor refused to marry my lover and me due to the untimely pregnancy, the final seal of disapproval. So I committed another unthinkable sin. We moved in together. I was making my own rules at this point, and my self-image plummeted. I felt like a fringe member of society. What kind of example was I setting for my then teenage children? I foolishly tried to pretend everything was fine, put on a happy face and hoped that that no one would notice this ramshackle life I was living.

I drifted further from the traditional roots of my childhood and began questioning the validity of the teachings and beliefs of my religion. How could a loving God condemn me for wanting to be loved? Didn't Jesus die for my sins? Were mine too terrible to be forgiven? My questions went on and on. I continued to go to church almost daily, seeking the answers to my questions. Deep in my heart I knew there must be answers that made sense. Then something wonderfully unexpected happened.

I visited another church, a very different kind of church, with a friend. I was looking for some contemporary music for our youth at my church. Little did I know this would turn out to be a date with destiny. I went looking for contemporary music, but I found so much more. It turned out to be a life-changing event.

First of all, the church was packed wall-to-wall. Everyone seemed happy to be there, unlike my church where we went out of duty fearing punishment if we missed. As the music began, the place erupted in joyful singing. And everyone sang, even the men! In my church, very few people actually engaged in the service. We just "did our time" and became fidgety if the service ran long.

As the music slowed to a more subdued level, I noticed nearly everyone had their eyes closed, hands lifted to heaven and seemed transported to another realm. I had never seen anything like this. These people knew something I didn't know. I wanted what they had and was determined to get it.

Week after week I returned. I would go to my church on Saturday evening and come to this new church on Sunday morning. After about six weeks of this, one Sunday morning I was standing in the back, hoping I could make it through the service without having to leave as my allergies were acting up badly.

Suddenly it was as if an internal screen appeared in my heart. I could see Jesus hanging on the cross. I had always known Jesus died so that we could be forgiven of our sins, but at that moment, I realized I was forgiven of my sins. He had paid the price for all my faults, failings and not measuring up. Oh, I get it! He was the Lamb of God offered as a sacrifice for sin, all sin, my sin, once and for all. I didn't have to earn it with good behavior like I believed all my life. He had done it. I was forgiven, guilt-free, and perfectly acceptable to God. I was free!

I felt as if the windows of my soul flew open, the sun shone in with a brilliant light. A fresh wind blew through, clearing out all the guilt, shame and condemnation that I felt from not measuring up. All the darkness inside evaporated in the presence of this wonderful light.

Such a burden of guilt was lifted from my heart that my appearance literally changed. Everyone I knew was shocked at the transformation in me. "Did you lose weight?" "Color your hair?" "Get a tan?" They couldn't figure out what it was. I was glowing from the inside out.

My external circumstances didn't change; in fact, things got worse after that, but my perception of myself changed 180 degrees. I now saw myself as God saw me, perfectly acceptable. No longer did I have to work for or earn God's approval. No longer did I have to worry if I would be good enough to "get into" heaven. I was adopted into the family of God. My future was sealed in a blood covenant between Jesus and God made on my behalf. Wow! What a gift!

I was free to live my life from approval rather than for approval. God had an adventure waiting for me, and life took on a new meaning. I had heaven on my side, and God was using every negative experience of my life for good in the lives of others. He took the shattered pieces of my makeshift life and created a masterpiece.

I'm still a work in progress and continually stand amazed at God's ability to use this fragile piece of clay to accomplish His work in the earth. But Jesus said we would do even greater things than He did. To those who believe he gives the right to become children of God, His Spirit takes up residence inside our hearts and works through us to bring heaven to earth. We can change the world, in spite of ourselves, in spite of our shortcomings, in spite of not measuring up when we surrender to the Lord. That is nothing short of miraculous.

I may be guilty, but through the blood of Jesus Christ, I am not charged!

Amy Hayes is an author, speaker and mother of eight children. She is passionate about helping parents raise successful kids. Her books include How I Raised 8 Amazing Kids in Spite of Myself and Parenting with Grace. In her spare time Ms. Hayes enjoys nature.

Thoughts to Ponder

from Guilty, but Not Charged

1. Your religion does not impress God; a relationship with Him does.

2. God wants us to strive for perfection, but knows we are not perfect.

3. God is the only perfect parent.

What kind of daily relationship do you have with your Heavenly Father?

Children's children are a crown to the aged, and parents are the pride of their children. — Proverbs 17:6
Children are a heritage from the Lord, offspring a reward from him. — Psalm 127:3

The Investigation
by David Lytle McDonough Sr.

A detective in a criminal investigation will look for three important considerations in determining whether a person could be a potential suspect. First, does the potential suspect have a *motive* to commit the crime in question; second, does the person have the *means* to commit this crime; and third, did the person in question have the *opportunity* to commit this crime.

Motive, means and opportunity were important in my life because they represented escape from the turbulent home life I experienced during my childhood. Constant arguing and alcohol created a challenging childhood I did not understand. I blamed myself, and believed if I could do things better or be better, the circumstances would change. I had no idea my parent's actions had nothing to do with me. Eventually realizing that "being good" could not change anything, I determined escaping the turbulent family would be the best answer.

My motive was to follow the path of my older brother and sister who made better grades than I did and were able to escape to prestigious eastern boarding schools, beginning in the eighth grade. My motive was strong, but the means and opportunity were weak, due to poor grades in school and low self-esteem.

Finally, a great opportunity came during my senior year in high school as I was applying for college admission. Most of the colleges I applied to rejected me because my grade point average placed me in the lower half of my graduating class. Then, I heard from a small out-of-state college located in Massachusetts. In the 60's the school admissions office was looking for out-of-state students, and being from Dallas, they were willing to loosen their entrance requirements a bit for me to get in. Motive, means, and opportunity were finally all coming together for my escape to any place far from home.

My get away motive was strong, and my opportunity finally arrived; but a big problem with my means came up. I was not getting scholarship money from this Massachusetts college, which meant that my Dad needed to pay for my education. He firmly believed if you were going to live and work in Texas, then you needed to attend a Texas college. I wanted to get away from Texas, so he told me that if I would go to any college in Texas for one year and do well, then he would pay for an out of state college. My means was gone, so I agreed to go to North Texas State University (NTSU) in Denton for a year. I still had motive, opportunity and eventually the means to make the escape I wanted. As life would have it, I actually began to like NTSU and Denton my first year. I was far enough away from home to be on my own and close enough to get back for holiday events.

Life moved on, and I stayed in Denton at North Texas, getting more lost in myself and the world. Four years passed with no degree, and suddenly something unexpected happened. The Military Selective Service lottery was established. My birthday lined up with a low lottery number, so off I went into the military. Being self-absorbed, I did not realize the miracle of getting into the United States Coast Guard (another testimony in itself). For the following four years I traveled throughout the Pacific and Asia, and various port cities in the U.S. I now had the escape I always wanted without any means, motive or opportunity. It just happened.

Because alcohol had been such a negative part of my growing up years, I made one of those personal vows never to drink. That worked during high school and college. Being overseas in Guam with a bunch of sailors, the vow I made quickly dissolved. It started with one beer at the Club Mocambo, the Enlisted Men's club on Guam, and continued on to a path of near destruction. That first drink was an act of defiance on my part.

After the Coast Guard, I completed college; after a short nine-month engagement, there was marriage. Life moved on with a successful career in commercial real estate, which led to a new motive, means and opportunity in my life. Wealth was the motive; and the means were long hours away from my family. This turned me into a man pleaser and led to more insecurity. Promotions provided opportunity with a variety of Texas and Florida companies. The trick to success (at least in my eyes) was to keep moving ahead of any potential problems with the companies I worked for or their commercial properties. This thinking also led to owning residential rental properties along with a thriving janitorial business at the end of my thirty-two year career.

The first fourteen years were the most turbulent because I had a young family and was working long hours. I drank alcohol to try to keep it all together and build my low self-esteem. My wife was not happy because she was caring for four young children by herself with very little support from me. Although everything looked good on the outside, my life and family were on a downward spiral.

My carnal life came to an abrupt end on December 19, 1990 after a very successful real estate year in Tampa, Florida. I was working for a Canadian company where our Florida commercial properties outperformed our projections. I was the Director of Commercial Real Estate for Florida at the time and because of our banner year, we decided to have a celebration. Although we planned a more formal event later with executives arriving from Toronto, December 19th was the celebration day in our Tampa office.

At my request, alcohol, without much food, began flowing around 3:00 p.m. as we were putting the final touches on our reports and accounting to be placed in overnight mail to the home office in Toronto. Care was taken to ensure the reports and accounting details were accurate before mailing because, as an office, we were proud of our accomplishments and wanted the home office to appreciate them as well.

The DHL currier came, the large bound reports were sent out, and we began the party. It started in our office and moved to a restaurant close by. After spending several hours partying, I left ahead of most of the others, who were now eating before they decided to drive home. I didn't need food. In my mind all I needed was to get home. In 1990, a drive home at 9:00 p.m. was a non-event activity in Tampa, Florida. However, with all of the Christmas parties and downtown events going on, the roads were busy.

As I drove through downtown Tampa, as I had done hundreds of other times, there was an event at the Performing Arts Center with lots of traffic. I was in no shape to drive and ended up running into the back of another car. A low-speed incident, it was no big deal. It turned out to be a huge deal because the driver I ran into saw my condition and flagged a nearby policeman, who promptly arrested me. I was quickly hauled off to a night in the Hillsborough (Tampa) county jail. My wife bailed me out the next morning, but prior to that I had all night to figure everything out. The plan was to profusely apologize, go home, shower, change and get back to the office where life would move on.

Nothing moved on at that point. On the way home from jail, we took a different route to a small town south of St. Petersburg called Largo, Florida. My wife informed me we were headed for Medfield Clinic in Largo, and I was going to sign myself in there or she was taking our children and moving back to Dallas. Everything was real clear at that point in my life. I was a mess, and I was about to lose my family. I was on the edge of feeling shame and remorse for my life, but that was to come later during the counseling portion at Medfield. I was where I swore I'd never be.

Have you ever felt that way?

My old motive, means and opportunity were abruptly ended. I was about to develop a whole new motive and the means and opportunity would follow.

While at Medfield, I was assigned to the Christian section of the Clinic and to a counselor, John Thompson, who was an associate Pastor of a non-denominational church in Tampa. He had a Doctorate in Theology, so he was known as Dr. Thompson. On our first interview, Dr. Thompson asked me if I was a Christian and if I knew that I was an alcoholic. He also asked, "Do you believe God can deliver you from alcohol?" My response to everything was yes. His response was, "No you don't. You are lying, and all you want is another drink." Then the shame and remorse came because Dr. Thompson was right. All I wanted was another drink.

Dr. Thompson explained that no real change could ever take place in my life without knowing Jesus Christ as my personal Lord and Savior. Years earlier I claimed to receive Jesus into my heart but that was mostly to please my Christian wife, Susan. There was no real change in my life, and all my heart wanted was life *my way*. After several weeks of counseling, I repented of my sins and surrendered my life to Jesus Christ as my personal Lord and Savior.

That first drink of defiance finally turned into total surrender.

Then Dr. Thompson asked me the same question as before. Did I believe that Jesus Christ could deliver me from alcohol? We prayed a short prayer. I'm thinking, should we pray a little longer? So, I asked him after his prayer, "Is that it?" He said, "That's it."

I was released from Medfield after several months and returned to work. By law, my employer had to hold my job, so I was anxious to get back to work and prove my value to the company so they wouldn't look for another way to fire me.

At first I didn't notice anything different because I was so immersed in family life and work. Then it occurred to me the desire for alcohol was actually gone. During the late afternoon and after work there was no desire for a drink of any kind except water or a soda. The miracle of being delivered by God struck me, and the reality was evident to everyone who knew me. I was excited about my transformation, but one thing still bothered me. My wife who had been so hurt was skeptical that my deliverance would last. It took time, but she eventually embraced the change in me, first through salvation, then through deliverance. She witnessed that I was spending more time with the family and less at the office. My priorities changed from work to family, and my job didn't suffer at all.

Last December of 2015 marked 25 years since I surrendered my life to Jesus Christ as Savior. God gives all mankind free will. I could have chosen either not to have signed myself into Medfield Clinic for help, or I could have rejected Christ while there. The need for change in my life was so strong that I could not have continued on any longer with my lifestyle. I was miserable, and those in my family who loved me were miserable.

You may be looking at your life and thinking that you would like changes, but you are not sure about how to begin. I can tell you from experience if I had not taken the free gift of God's grace into my life, I might not be here today. I might not be alive.

God created all of us and has a perfect plan for our lives, but we cannot discover His plan for our lives unless we surrender our lives to God's Son, Jesus Christ. John 3:16 tells us that, "For God so loved the world that He gave His only Son, that whoever believes in Him should not perish, but have eternal life." That eternal life means going to Heaven after death and living with Christ forever in the family of God.

As a Christian, motive, means and opportunity have a whole new meaning. The motive is to honor and please God through obedience to His Word and surrender to His will in my life. The means is repenting of my sins and receiving Jesus Christ into my life as Lord and Savior. A daily rededication and thankfulness for God's grace in my life, along with time alone with Jesus in His Word keeps me close to Him. The opportunity is now. God created all mankind with the free will to accept His offer of salvation and allow God to fulfill His plan for this world through us.

Have you ever conducted an investigation of your life, examining the motives behind your behavior? Ask God to show you how he sees you. He will give you the means and opportunity to change.

David McDonough serves in the Prison Ministry program at Prestonwood Baptist Church. He was born in Dallas, and graduated from the University of North Texas after serving in the U.S. Coast Guard. He is now retired in Plano, Texas with his wife of forty years. They have four children and four grandchildren.

Thoughts to Ponder

from The Investigation

1. God disciplines His children.

2. We all have needs that cannot be met by anyone or anything other than God.

3. We must not allow peer pressure to move us off God's plumb line.

When has God saved you from yourself?

Do not get drunk on wine, which leads to debauchery. Instead, be filled with the Spirit. — Ephesians 5:18

Once an Ugly Duckling
by Amy Morgan

Have you heard the story of the ugly duckling? You might remember hearing it when you were growing up. To paraphrase, much to mother duck's surprise, one of her ducklings doesn't fit in. It doesn't look like its brothers and sisters, and it doesn't act like the other ducklings. It is awkward, thought to be ugly, and out of place.

But low and behold, one day it discovers it's not a duckling, but a swan, not awkward and out of place, but created differently and beautifully to be its own unique creature.

Growing up, I felt like the ugly duckling. Can anybody relate? I was told at a young age I was adopted, and although my parents made it very clear they loved me and chose me, I struggled to feel like I fit into the family, and consequently in life.

My adoptive parents, as well as all the relatives, were quiet and reserved. There was not a lot of room or patience for a bouncy, outgoing, talkative little girl. I wanted to be affirmed, seen, and delighted in. Instead, I was told to shush.

My home was not happy growing up. My dad, a successful doctor, struggled and still struggles, with alcoholism and work-a-holism. He drifted in and out of our home. Although we didn't have a name for it then, my younger sister has mental illness. All of this created turmoil and a real lack of emotional connection between my family members and me.

My insecurities grew when my father backed away from the family early in my childhood. My parents didn't officially divorce, but he moved out of the house, leaving me feeling abandoned and alone. My mother was lonely and unhappy.

She devoted herself to work at church and teaching pre-school, but there was little joy in her life. I did not want to be sad like she was, so I resolved to make my own way.

Have any of you ever walked down that path? You feel like your life is out of control, like you don't fit in? So by golly, you make a life for yourself where you do fit in. One of my mottos used to be, "God helps those who help themselves."

Like my dad, I looked really good on the outside. Varsity runner, cheerleader, academic scholarship to college, everything the world says equals success; but inside, I never felt like I was good enough. If I could just perform a little better, be thinner or prettier, then I'd find someone to love me, I'd fit in and find the place and purpose I wanted in the world.

Have any of you felt like that? Abandoned, lost, lonely, desperately trying to control everything in your world, and feeling it all slipping from your grasp. No ability to authentically connect emotionally with anyone. I still felt like an ugly duckling on the inside. Well, you can guess where all that led: serial boyfriends, drinking, perfectionism and self-control. Through college and my early twenties, my loneliness grew, and my self-destructive behavior escalated.

I looked polished and professional on the outside until the inner poison bubbled out in my mid-twenties. I made a series of very bad choices, and I was exposed, humiliated, and rejected. My family heaped shame upon me. When people saw I wasn't as together as they wanted to believe, I was abandoned, shamed, and left alone. Have you ever been there? Have you ever been kicked when you are down?

There's something else you should know about me. I'm a runner. I think God knew I needed to run away, my own way, until I reached the end of my abilities. I realized I ran myself into a situation I couldn't fix, so it forced me to look toward my Heavenly Father.

I found myself at a crossroads. I could run to God, or away from Him. And thankfully, this time I realized I needed to turn in the opposite direction and run to God. I knew the right choice because I had heard all the stories about God's forgiveness and how his Son, Jesus's, sacrifice on the cross would fill the insecurities and sadness I felt deep inside of me.

He paid for those sins I racked up in my account, all the bad choices I made that hurt others and myself. All I needed to do was tell him I was sorry and ask Him to help me not go down that road again. I chose to believe in Jesus, trust him and ask Him to help me live in a different way, to run a different direction—one that was decent, and good, and gave me peace and self-worth.

I stepped forward, and honestly looked at what I had done, and opted to change. I faced the consequences of my actions, some of which still followed me. But feelings of shame are not from God. The more I live a life pursuing things that are good and decent, helpful and right, and things I learned by studying the most important book in the world, the Bible, the more I can be at peace.

God does not reject me. I am not alone. I am not forever dirty and damaged. I fit in, and I can hold my head up.

I don't have to keep trying to be the perfect duck. I can be the swan God made me to be. And once I turned to God for fulfillment, rather than try to manufacture it on my own, God gave me a wonderful gift.

He led me to find my birth parents and to share my story, encouraging others about the great gift of life.

Thirteen years ago, I didn't even know I wanted to find my birth parents, but then I came across a notice in a parenting magazine that mentioned adoption records had been opened in Kansas (where I was born and raised). I squirreled that scrap of paper away in my Day-Timer and carried it around for six years. Subsequently, I married and had two little boys.

I was grieved that I didn't have a daughter, and I thought about adopting a little girl, maybe from China or Korea. One day my husband told me that if we were meant to adopt a child, he believed he would have that desire too, and he didn't. He looked right at me and said he thought, instead, that I was the little girl. My desire was not to have a daughter, but to be the daughter. It felt as if a light bulb had gone off. He was right!

I pulled the scrap of paper out, miraculously still tucked into a pocket of my Day-Timer, and called the records office in Topeka, Kansas. They not only still had my file with my original birth certificate, they connected me to the social work office, which had other records. I now knew the names of my birth parents and the address where my birthmother's parents lived.

I took a trip to Kansas, picked up the paperwork, and drove to the address listed. The house was vacant and for sale. But it looked like what I call a "grandma" house, one where people might have lived and been part of the community for a while. So I knocked on the next-door neighbor's door, explaining that I was a relative doing some research. Not only had they known the people who would have been my birth-grandparents, they saved some yearbooks of my birthmother's brother. As they handed them to me, I looked at the very first picture I'd ever seen of a blood relative. I felt chills run down my arms.

And then, miraculously, the neighbor returned from the other room with a yellowed newspaper clipping from several years previous, an obituary for my birthmother's mother, who had been a second grandmother to the neighbor's children. The clipping revealed my birthmother's married name—another step closer. The name was very unusual. On my first call, I reached her brother-in-law, who forwarded my information to her.

I always fantasized about my birth parents. Who they'd be and what they'd look like. I'd always wanted to know my heritage and ancestry. Did I have half siblings? I steeled myself for more rejection. After all, they had given me up. There was a reason for that. Maybe someone assaulted my birthmother. Maybe my birth parents were awful! What would I find?

Barely two weeks after starting my quest, I found myself sitting in my birthmother's living room in the southern suburbs of Kansas City, just one school district south of the one in which I had grown up. She told me her story and confirmed my birthfather's information. He attended a boy's prep school where eighteen years later I would be invited to prom, the one he and my birthmother had missed because, by then, she was well advanced into her pregnancy with me.

She told me they had been high school sweethearts. After dating several years, one thing led to another, resulting in an unplanned pregnancy. Things weren't easy for an unwed couple in the conservative Midwest, even in the mid-60s. She was living in a dorm as she pursued career training after high school. Her parents told her not to come home; they didn't want her younger brothers to see her pregnant. They did not support her emotionally or financially.

Fortunately, she said my birthfather stuck by her. Partially because of his Catholic upbringing, he encouraged her to deliver me and place me for adoption. My birthfather was living on his own during his senior year of high school. He was present at the hospital when I was delivered, and he made it a point to see me and say goodbye.

I was born a few short years before Roe vs. Wade; abortion was still illegal in the United States in 1967. My birthmother saw, first-hand, the results of illegal abortions working at the hospital—and didn't need too much convincing to avoid that route, despite the physical and emotional difficulties of the pregnancy.

My birthmother worked and attended school at the very same medical school hospital where my adopted father was a medical resident. Who knows, the two may have passed each other in the halls, never knowing that the child in her growing belly would be the daughter he would adopt.

An OB/GYN physician at the medical school was the go-between. He provided medical care for my birthmother's unplanned pregnancy, and he knew my father and mother wanted a child. A private adoption was arranged and handled properly through the state of Kansas system. Five days after delivery, my parents came home from the hospital with their baby girl, me.

My birth parents continued dating, but drifted apart during the next few years. He followed his dreams to build a career out West, married later and had children. She did the same, wisely waiting to start a family until she was settled and could raise her children as she had hoped.

My birthmother lost touch with my birthfather by the time I met her, but God intervened again. I walked into the records department of his former high school on a Saturday afternoon in the summer. For some reason, the alumni relations director was there and cheerfully handed me a printout of all my birthfather's information. Now I could contact him.

I returned home and placed the phone call. After exchanging information, my birthfather said words that would impact me for the rest of my life: "What took you so long? I've been waiting for you for 36 years." At that moment, I felt such an overwhelming rush of love and healing. I felt like I had been lost and was now found, like the story of the prodigal son who is warmly embraced by his father upon his return to his family. And the feeling was mutual. In fact, my elder son shares his first name with my birthfather, something we did not know when we named him six years prior to our knowing each other.

I truly feel that God used the reconnection of family ties and the love of an earthly birthfather to teach me about the depths of His love for each and every one of His children.

Later, my birthfather invited me to meet his entire extended family, including his 84-year-old mother, who had not known about my existence. At one point, the whole gathering, from the smallest grandchild to the oldest grandma, started dancing around the house, pulling out hats and loudly requesting favorite songs. I was astounded! These were my people! I wasn't the overly demonstrative, talkative child who needed to shush. I fit in.

Again, huge waves of love, affirmation and belonging crashed over me. I went outside and looked at the sky. God painted a beautiful sunset over the house in my favorite color, coral pink. I knew He was telling me I was beloved, and I could tangibly feel it.

I am eternally grateful and thankful to my birth parents for *choosing life*, for making the difficult decision to go ahead with an unplanned and problematic pregnancy. They are delightful people, and I am so grateful that the Lord opened the doors for me to find and connect with them at the age of thirty-six. I have great peace and comfort filling in the gaps of my story, my history, my genealogy, and my genetics.

If you want to know how I feel about my parents and my birth parents, please know, love multiplies; it doesn't divide. Nothing replaces my relationship with my adoptive parents. They are my parents. Sure they made mistakes, but haven't we all? I am grateful the Lord put me with them in a Christian home where I was loved and cared for. I am grateful for the love and care they've given me. And any child would feel the same, eternally grateful for the sacrifice and greater love of being chosen.

A yet-to-be born baby growing inside is a person just like me. I work part-time and, following the footsteps of all members of my family, biological and adopted, give back to society in many ways as a volunteer. Both nurture and influence the person I am.

I realize now how valuable my life is as evidenced by the service God calls me to: every meal I make to serve the homeless or elderly or impoverished; every article I write sharing how God is working in our community; every family I've touched through prayer group leadership; every widow in Rwanda I've visited, encouraged and supported; every soul I've led to Christ through teaching Sunday School or Bible study; every Ugandan child who's found hospitality in my home; and yes, every cookie I've baked and carpool mile I've driven. What would have been lost if my life had been deemed worthless or too inconvenient to continue?

No matter how messy, *life* is always the right choice. God works all things for good; he makes beauty from the ashes. What seems like a tragedy today can be a triumph in the future. Through the power of the Holy Spirit, ugly ducklings are transformed into swans.

Amy Morgan graduated from TCU with a journalism degree. She writes, edits, and works in public relations. Amy serves in many volunteer capacities and was recognized in 2015 as a PTA Life Member. She is running a half marathon supporting clean water in Africa, where she travelled in 2014. Texasmorgans4@sbcglobal.net.

Thoughts to Ponder
from Once an Ugly Duckling

1. You have been designed by God.

2. Regardless of your earthly family, as a believer we are adopted into God's family.

3. When we are connected to God, He will connect us to others.

What does being a part of God's family mean to you?

He predestined us for adoption to sonship through Jesus Christ, in accordance with his pleasure and will. — Ephesians 1:5

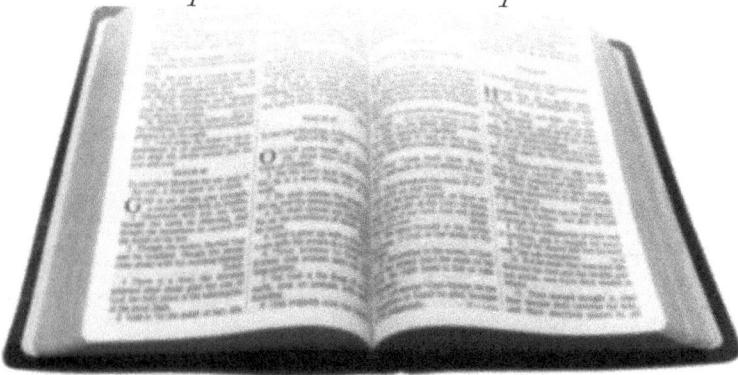

Voiceless

by Jeanne Nigro

Have you ever experienced feelings of nervousness or fear when getting up to speak in front of others? Trust me, I understand how you feel. Believe it or not, even though I love to teach and enjoy speaking in front of others, it didn't used to be that way. In fact, I would be so afraid to speak in front of others that I would literally start to black out and lose consciousness.

I remember in college when I presented case studies in graduate school, I couldn't look at anyone in the eye, I would look away, and I would lose my voice. It would just flat out disappear! I would start to sweat, get dizzy, see all white, and then all black and start to faint. I used to change majors based on whether or not they had a speech requirement. Speech class felt like a fate worse than death, and no major was worth that.

Why did I react that way? What was behind all of those symptoms of losing consciousness? How did I get to where I am now where I love to speak in front of others? Behind it all was the fear of being exposed; that everyone would see how bad, how inadequate and what a failure I really was inside.

Growing up the youngest of seven kids, I received a lot of messages that told me (or that I interpreted to mean) that I was bad, inadequate, and that I didn't have a voice. In fact, I didn't even feel I had a right to exist, so I quickly learned the best thing for me to do was to be invisible. I barely spoke growing up. My mom used to take me to throat specialists all the time because I literally did not have a voice. I believed in my heart so strongly I didn't have the right to have a voice, that it actually manifested itself in my body as no audible voice. I believed I had some sort of defect, that something was wrong with me because I couldn't talk. Everyone always said to me, "You're so shy!" I truly thought it was a disease I was born with and would have to endure the rest of my life. I didn't understand then what was behind it. When we are young, we assume we are the problem.

It was like this all the way through grade school, but then in high school I found a way to express, or get that voice out, and that was through drinking. I found when I drank, I could freely express myself for the first time in my life, and it was very liberating. In fact, I became so good at it I prided myself on being able to outdrink anyone, and I could. I was quite the party girl from the time I was about sixteen to twenty-eight years old.

Another interesting thing I discovered in high school was that I felt good about myself and determined I had worth and value if I could get a man sexually attracted to me. I learned the bar pick-up scene, and I excelled in it. By the time I rented my first apartment at age twenty-two, Cosmopolitan magazine was my handbook for daily living. All of its articles told me how I was to act with men and how to make decisions about life and career; but unfortunately, it didn't go into any detail about all the pain, rejection, and hopelessness that resulted from the lifestyle it promoted.

By the time I was in my mid-twenties, I was out of college and trying to find my way in life; I felt extremely lost, hopeless and lonely. I searched for true meaning and purpose in life, *what my heart was into* and what I was created for. I moved out to Southern California after graduate school thinking I would find "truth" and the meaning of life there. I actually believed people were more enlightened in California than they were in the Midwest.

I changed jobs and careers as often as every two months. With each move, I felt more and more empty, desperate and hopeless in my quest to find something I believed in and that gave me purpose and meaning in life. I drank even more excessively (if that was even possible) and became more promiscuous, picking up men from bars almost nightly. I was desperately searching for love, to feel valued and that I had worth to men; however, I was definitely looking in all the wrong places. I experienced tremendous shame, self-condemnation, loneliness and physical pain, enduring horrible surgeries due to STDs, (sexually transmitted diseases). I remember being in a hospital after almost hemorrhaging to death and looking out the window wanting to jump out. I was completely alone, and found no comfort or love in this world.

Again, the lies and messages of the world I had followed never advertised the physical consequences or the shame and rejection that followed those consequences. I felt worthless and unlovable. I lost hope that I would ever find someone to love me.

Within a period of nine months, I ended up having three surgeries and two car accidents. Because of my mounting medical expenses, my health insurance plan dropped me. At the time, I was working two part-time jobs and doing two internships toward a master's in psychology. This change in health insurance forced me to look for a full-time job that offered the benefits I needed for all of these medical bills.

One day, I met a guy riding his bike in the alley near the beach. He was wearing an Ohio State sweatshirt. We became "drinking buddies." He submitted my resume to his employer, McDonnell Douglas, in Long Beach, California. Eventually I was hired at Douglas, but I resisted accepting the offer because I was a "new ager" at the time and was vehemently opposed to anything related to the defense industry. I actually believed if we all just thought "peaceful thoughts," the cosmic consciousness of the world would live in peace, similar to the John Lennon song, "Imagine."

I ended up accepting the job, forced by the need for medical benefits, but with my own understanding that I would just take it for a month or two while I continued to interview for other jobs that *my heart was into* and that were consistent with my core new age beliefs.

I was hired at McDonnell Douglas to implement an organizational change initiative within their Marketing department; however, the Vice-President of Marketing was not yet open to this strategy, so I and four others on the team, who were hired to implement this initiative in other areas of the company, had nothing to do for six months. When have you ever heard of that happening in a company? Never!

One of the others who was hired was a born again Christian. From day one I determined to stay far from him as I always did with Christians because they were always trying to convert me. I wanted nothing to do with them or their forced conversions. I thought they were all uneducated, loser, nut cases. However, this guy (Rich) was different because he didn't try to force his faith on me; he was actually a true friend to me. I had no experience in the job I was hired for (again, how often does that happen? Never!), and he helped me in so many practical ways, both at work and outside of work with things like moving, helping with my car, all the things that single women in California with no family have desperate need of.

Over the next six months, we spent many hours debating about God. I threw out every CD or handout he gave me about God. However, he never judged me or told me what to do, but would listen to all of my stories and ask questions, leaving me to think and discover truth for myself. Eventually, he did succeed in encouraging me to listen to

Christian Psychology radio programs. I was amazed that psychological truths could actually be found in the Bible. Again, I thought the Bible was only for the uneducated. On Christmas Eve of that year, Rich and his family invited me to a Christmas Eve service. I agreed because I wanted to hear Christmas carols. Who doesn't like Christmas carols, regardless of whether or not you believe in God? I'll never forget when the Pastor said that Jesus was the first Christmas gift (sent by God) and how would I feel if I bought someone a Christmas gift they wouldn't open? I spent the day shopping for Rich and his family and thought about how I would feel. I never heard Jesus put in that context before, and it penetrated my heart.

Three months later, I turned twenty-eight years old. By this time, everything had come to a head in my life. I could not find my purpose. I started to believe I didn't have one. I couldn't find someone to love me. All I experienced was rejection and being used for sex—even by a psychologist friend I thought would be the ultimate, all together guy. I couldn't overcome feelings of worthlessness, even though I had been through five years of therapy. By that point, I understood all of my issues and family dysfunctions in my head; however, I couldn't change how I really felt about myself deep down in my heart.

At work, I ended up in a room full of older VP-level men that I was supposed to facilitate through a re-organization process. They were finally ready to implement the change initiative in Marketing because the entire organization was being forced to do it. Well guess what happened to my voice? That's right, I couldn't speak. I sat there for five hours (that's how long the daily meetings were) and couldn't say a word. I felt too worthless. Those old messages came back. I had nothing valuable or important to say, I was inadequate, stupid, worthless, I didn't have a right to exist; I didn't have a voice in the midst of these high-level men. Basically, I was sitting in a room full of my older brothers.

That night in my apartment, I felt hopeless in every area of my life: career, finding purpose, overcoming worthlessness, being rejected by men, feeling unlovable, being unable to change. I wanted to die, and I thought about how I might end my life. I no longer could bare the pain of living; all I knew was that I just wanted the pain to end. Have you ever felt that way?

I was lying on my bed wanting to end my life because I felt that was the only way to stop the pain, and that there was no hope of ever changing. I felt totally rejected, unwanted, and a worthless failure. I hadn't believed in God throughout my twenties; but because I was listening to Christian radio, and occasionally attending services with Rich, I thought I'd make one last plea. I said God, "If you are real, take control of my life because I don't want it anymore." I didn't even understand then who He was or what His Son, Jesus, had done for me. I cried out in my desperation and He heard my heart and accepted me just as I was. The next day I went into work, and I had strength and a feeling of worth that I had never experienced before. I ended up being the top facilitator at McDonnell Douglas in the months that followed.

That was twenty-seven years ago, March 20, 1989. Since then I've gained a better understanding that even though He was God in the flesh, He loved me. He wanted me so badly that He willingly died for me so His blood would cover me and make me acceptable, just as I was, to God. Even in my sin, I could have an intimate relationship with a holy and perfect God, now and forever, not based on how good I am, but all based on what Jesus did for me. Everything I had done wrong all those years, all of that shame that I carried for all of the bad things I'd done and for just growing up feeling that I was bad and something was wrong with me was all washed away, cleansed and forgiven.

Since that time, I've experienced true love in Him. Only God can love me 100 percent perfectly all of the time. Only He will never reject me and never put me down. Only He can give me worth, a new identity, purpose and meaning in life. He actually desires me, delights in me and enjoys being with me! His heart is ravished toward me. He can't take His eyes off of me, and He can't stop thinking about me! He is the love I have been searching for all of my life. I never have to feel unwanted, bad, or worthless again. I'm now doing what *my heart is into*, what I believe in, helping others to know this amazing God who has redeemed my life from the pit and crowned me with love and compassion.

Everything I am, everything I have today is a result of His grace, mercy and love in my life. To top it off, He has given me a voice, a strong voice to speak for Him all around the country. I love public speaking. Now that's a miracle! He also gave me a loving husband.

Life hasn't been perfect these past twenty-seven years. When my daughter was born fifteen years ago, she had special needs; basically had a breakdown, spiritually, mentally, physically, and emotionally. I believed the lie that God had abandoned me. He has since healed my heart and showed me He was with me all along and that He was crying, too. Any time since I gave my life to God that has been difficult or that I have struggled, it's always been because I have either believed a lie about myself or about Him. Usually both, because they go arm in arm. God has never left me, and He has never stopped loving me; in fact, it's impossible for Him to do so. His love is like the sunshine; it can't stop radiating. Now the clouds (or lies we believe in our heart about ourselves or Him) may block us from feeling His love, but it never stops coming toward us. His love is like fire, a jealous, passionate, consuming fire. Fire advances through any obstacle; nothing can stand in its way, and such is His love toward us. Nothing, not even our weakness or failures can stop His love from coming toward us. We are beautiful to Him even in our weakness, because when God sees us, He sees us as the perfect, finished product.

Experiencing His love and intimate relationship with Him is our very purpose for living, and it's the only thing that can never change. It can never be taken away from us. I am so thankful I asked God to take control of my life on that desperate night in my apartment in Seal Beach, California. He truly redeemed my life from the pit and crowned me with love and compassion. He took me from "death to life."

My passion in ministry now comes from the healing work that God has done in my life. I desire to help others grow in the intimacy with God that has made such a dramatic difference in my own life. There is no higher calling, and there is nothing else in life that I would rather be doing than this. At last, after all of those years of searching for the meaning of life, I have found my purpose for living, *what my heart is into*. I found it in glorifying God, acknowledging that my life belongs to Him and that His desire and my purpose is to experience intimacy with Him every minute of the day.

Jeanne Nigro, a seasoned author, teacher, and television personality, empowers thousands around the globe to stand strong in these uncertain times through a more intimate relationship with God. Jeanne's passion, powerfully communicated in her book, UNSHAKEN, is mobilizing her audiences to fulfill their God-given purpose for these times. www.jeannenigro.com

Thoughts to Ponder
from Voiceless

1. God created our voices to speak.

2. God intended our bodies to be holy and house His Holy Spirit.

3. Satan is the enemy of our souls and he is a liar.

What gets between you and God?

Jesus said to them: "Watch out that no one deceives you." — Mark 13:5

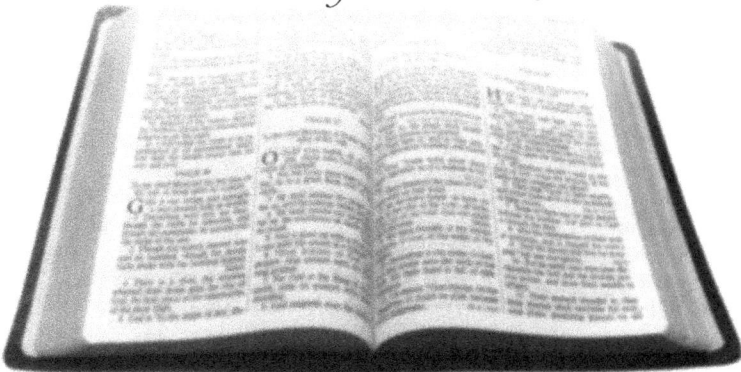

A Birthmother's Secret

by Brenda Mahon

"As pregnant as can be," said the doctor. Those were the most frightening words in the world for an 18-year-old high-school graduate who had hopes and dreams for the future. Now, hope came crashing down.

I changed my schedule at work for the following Sunday and went to church. I had not been to church in a while, but now a tragedy happened in my life. Where could I go but to God? While we were singing a song about the love of Jesus, I started weeping and couldn't stop. Tears flowed, dripping out onto the pages of the hymn book as I cried out, "Oh, God, why? How could this happen to me?" I was repentant and sorry I disappointed my Heavenly Father. In His loving, tender mercy, He spoke to my heart, "I will never leave you or forsake you. I will not give you more than you can handle."

I was a frightened young woman, but knowing God was with me brought comfort to my soul. I attended Sunday school, church and Vacation Bible School all of my younger years and accepted the Lord as my Savior at a young age, trusting Him completely. I felt His ever-loving presence and believed He was working good out of a very difficult situation. He was using my strong body to have a baby for someone who could not have one for themselves. He reminded me this was his baby, not mine.

I was eight months pregnant before my parents knew, and by then, I decided adoption was the best option for me and for the baby. My mom and dad were very supportive of the decision that I made and helped me the last month of my pregnancy before the baby was born. The very next day my mother drove me out to Fort Worth to the Gladney Home for Unwed Mothers. It was old and dreary looking and a long way from our home in north Dallas, but I knew that was what I had to do.

That evening when my dad came home from work, he told us about another option he learned about from the homeowner of the house he was remodeling. The homeowner knew a doctor and an attorney who helped with private adoptions. I had a meeting with the attorneys and learned the family would rent an apartment, not too far from our neighborhood, pay my bills and provide a weekly allowance for food and other needs I might have. They agreed to let me stay with my present doctor. They promised they would place the baby in a fine Christian home. Records would be sealed, and I would have no fear of anyone ever finding out about what happened to me.

No one else in my family knew about this, except for one brother who came to stay with me in the apartment until the baby was born. When I went into labor, my mother came late at night to take me to the hospital. The attorneys contacted the hospital to reserve a spot for me and called my mom to give her directions for where to take me. I had a late-term baby, born eleven days after his due date. Baylor Hospital did everything they could to hide my secret from the world. It was a difficult delivery, but finally the baby was born around 7 p.m. the next evening. I awoke in the recovery room crying like a baby for my mother.

They took me to a private room in the back of the maternity ward and didn't allow me to see the baby. In the early afternoon, the attorneys arrived with papers for me to sign. They gave me a box of chocolates and told me to go on with my life and forget it ever happened. Can a mother forget her unborn child? I don't think so. All I could do was cry. I didn't know if I had a boy or a girl. They would not tell me anything. Later my doctor told me I had a baby boy, weighing 7 lbs., 14 oz. That is all I was told.

Shortly after giving birth, I cried out to God again. Knowing how frightening this was and how easily it can happen, I asked God to bring someone into my life who would love and marry me.

Six weeks later, my sister and her husband who knew nothing about my crisis pregnancy and giving birth just a few weeks before, called and told me I was going to go out with them. They wanted to introduce me to a friend that went to school with Jim, my brother-in-law. I didn't want to go on a date, but she argued with me and told me to be ready at 7 p.m. that evening. We made arrangements to meet across town at the store where Jim was working. Eddie Mahon met us there. We all went out on the town, but I wasn't very impressed with him and didn't think we would date again. But the Lord had other plans. Eddie called and apologized to me for his bad behavior on the first date and asked me to give him another chance. That impressed me. So he picked me up for a date the following week and brought me back home an hour later; then asked me out again the following week.

Several dates later, Eddie took me out to dinner. Something about him was different. He also saw something in me he liked, and his conversation revolved around trying to get to know me. I was quiet and reserved, and he was having a hard time extracting much, if anything out of me.

Then he asked me what I wanted out of life. I said, "I don't know. What do you want?" His reply astounded me. He said, "I want to get married and have a family that goes to Sunday school and church together." In my heart, I rolled my eyes up toward God and said with a smirk, *This is the man that you have brought into my life.* I instantly remembered the prayer I prayed at twelve years old in the back of the church, when I couldn't be baptized because my parents were not there. I prayed, *God, when I grow up and get married, I want a man who will go to Sunday school and church with his family.* I had not given much thought to that prayer in years, but God never quit thinking about it. Just at the right moment, He brought us together. What an amazing God we serve! Eddie and I were married six months later, and I went on with my life of secrecy, never finding a way to tell Eddie what had happened. For years, I had difficulty even talking to God about it.

I never quit thinking about my baby boy and never really thought I would meet him or know him this side of heaven, but I wanted to make sure I would meet him in heaven. I was told he went to a fine Christian family. As I matured in my faith, I knew that being in a Christian family didn't make him a Christian. So I started praying, "Lord, if he doesn't know you as his personal Lord and Savior, I pray that someone will be brought into his life who can tell him about Jesus."

I held all of this in my heart for many years, just pondering it, not knowing what to do with this deep, dark secret I carried around for twenty-plus years. Every time I would hear the song, *I Surrender All*, my heart was heavily burdened. I wanted God to have all of me, but I didn't know how to surrender. After all, no one would ever know by looking at me that I was hiding a secret in my heart from the ones closest to me.

Years later, *The Cinderella Syndrome* was the topic of the Ladies' Night Out at one of the large churches here in town. The author of the book was speaking. I thought my two younger daughters, who were eighteen, twenty and single, as well as two sisters who were divorced, would benefit from this topic. I was looking forward to hearing what she had to say myself. What happened that night surprised me. The author spoke about her ordeal when she was a young woman. One of the employees at her work invited her to a party at his home. She arrived, but no one else showed up. She was attacked and raped that evening. Later, she found out she was pregnant and chose adoption. She went on to tell about her recent reunion with her daughter, who had gone on a search for her birth mother in the mid-eighties.

Her story was eerily similar to mine, and it made me nervous. There had already been many reunions, televised in the eighties. Adoptees from the sixties were reuniting with birth mothers and birth fathers. They were very heartwarming reunions, with much weeping and exhilaration. In the midst of my anxiety, I noticed a light shining brightly from the ceiling of this huge church. It appeared to point toward me, and I knew then God was pursuing me. I quickly excused myself, saying I was not feeling very well. Actually, I really was not feeling well; I thought I was going to have a nervous breakdown. I got out of the building as quickly as I could, and took off running to my car as though I was trying to outrun God. All the way I was saying, "Oh, God, what are you doing? What are you doing?" I knew this was the day!

I grabbed the open door, jumped in and gripped tightly to my steering wheel trying to hang on, not letting go. But the Lord God said, "Let me have this, Brenda. Give it to me." There was an inner dialogue going on that was causing me to question whether I could even trust God. I asked myself, *Can I even trust God?* Immediately, a small still voice said, *"Of course you can trust God."* At that moment, I let go of my grip on the steering wheel of my life and lifted my hands up to him and said, *Here, take this! I can't handle it anymore. I trust you.* I had no idea what He would do with it, but I felt at peace as I drove out of that parking lot to go home, and then I looked up and said to the Lord, "Remember, Eddie doesn't know about this."

138

It was out of this act of obedience in trusting God completely that I experienced a tender, loving, compassionate God who was real and personal. He had been very patient, guiding and directing my every step.

Just a few months later, after almost 25 years of not knowing anything except that I had given birth to a baby boy, I received a phone call. The sweet young female voice on the phone asked me, "Does April 30, 1964, mean anything to you?" I was speechless. And, then she said, "Your son is standing right here. Would you like to talk to him?" I said, "No, I do not want to talk to him, I want to see him." I gave them my office address, but couldn't give them directions. I was too nervous and excited. At the same time, I had doubts and questions about what it would be like and how it would affect my family. I wondered how he might feel knowing that I had "given him up."

How had my decision affected his life?

What would he want to say to me?

Would he be angry?

My emotions were all over the place. That Friday afternoon in my office, I had the privilege of meeting this young man named Mac for the first time. It was shocking! I never thought of him as a man. In walked a 6' 3", 200-pound football player. He was incredibly handsome. I could not take my eyes off of him.

For me, it was like a business meeting, no crying and weeping. I was simply glad to meet him. I invited Mac and his beautiful wife, Daryl, to sit down and talk for a while. The first thing he said to me was, "I want to thank you for not aborting me." Then he went on to tell me about his wonderful parents, his great life in Florida, and his love for football. He wanted to know about his conception and what happened to his birth father. He had been told all of his life that his birth father played football for the Houston Oilers, another fabricated story, probably by the attorneys, who wanted to appease the mother who was a huge football fan. Supposedly as the birth mother, I was an airline stewardess with American Airlines, far from the truth. I shared with him the Lord knew him before he was even conceived and had an exciting plan for his life. He seemed somewhat fascinated by all of this, but shared with me that he didn't know anything about Christ and never had been told any Bible stories.

It was then I knew God, in his infinite wisdom, chose me to be that "someone" that I had prayed years for, someone who could tell him about Jesus. Never in my wildest imagination did I think God would choose me to be the one to birth him into the Kingdom of God. As I swirled around in my chair to catch my breath, I heard a soft chuckle. I said, "Oh God, you are something else." I think He likes showing off! He is an amazing God who truly works all things to our good. "And we know that for those who love God all things God work together for good, for those who are called according to his purpose" (Romans 8:28).

I went home after dropping this sweet couple off at a hotel, so I could tell my husband Eddie what God had done that day. He was shocked when I told him what happened. He stood up and walked over to me and said, "Brenda, we've been married almost twenty-five years now. What else have you not told me?" I was crying and trembling. I knew this would be difficult for him and for me. I said, "What could be worse than this, Eddie? I have nothing else that I am holding on to." He asked where he was, and I told him, "I took him and his wife to a hotel, so I could come home and talk to you. I could not hold on to this any longer. I had to tell you, Eddie." Eddie thought for a moment and then said, "Well, if he is a son of yours, he doesn't belong in a hotel. So, let's go get him." That's exactly what we did. We had a nice evening getting acquainted.

The fun began early the next morning, introducing him to his granddad and grandmother, and calling our three girls, who were twenty, twenty-two and twenty-four years old, to tell them about the brother they didn't know they had. They all had different reactions. We called Sheila, our eldest who lived in New England, two thousand miles from home. All she could do was cry. She didn't like not being the oldest sibling anymore. Christy, our youngest didn't like it at all. Cynthia, our middle daughter, couldn't wait to meet him. She always wanted a brother.

It was an exciting time in our lives. My five brothers and three sisters were all amazed at the good news. I was fearful of calling my oldest brother. I thought he would be angry with me for giving a child away. So, I called him at work to tell him what had happened. I did all of the talking and then he said, "Thank you for calling me." That's all he said. Later that evening, he called me and said, "That's the most beautiful story I have ever heard. Have I told you lately how much I love you?" I received many loving calls, cards, and letters congratulating me and welcoming this young man into our family. What a surprise that was. I didn't expect that kind of reception at all. Eddie told me we were experiencing a miracle from a loving God, and others were astounded by it as well. Amazing!

Mac and his wife, Daryl, left to go back to their home in Florida, and we continued to talk on the phone every day. We connected them with a minister in Florida. They got involved with church and both of them were baptized. Eddie and I went to the baptism. The next day Mac took me to meet his adopted Dad. He was in the kitchen with his back to us as we walked through the front door. He was a silver-haired man, my parent's age, and when he turned around and looked at me, I thought I was looking into the face of God. I thought of the sacrifice Jesus made by shedding His own blood and adopting me into His household. All I could do was tremble.

We went into the den, and Mac handed me a photo album. Mac, at one day old, Mac at three days old, Mac at ten months old. The album was full of pictures of Mac in his childhood and early teens. I tried to not bond with this baby inside of me, and didn't think of him as my baby; consequently, I never grieved over the loss of this child. But that day, in his father's house, the floodgates were opened, and I shed a bucket load of tears. It was cleansing to my soul.

The following year I went on my own search to find the man who had gotten me pregnant. I don't like using the word "rape," but that's what happened that night. He had refused to take responsibility; he told me all he would do was pay for an abortion. I left that day and never looked back. I knew I couldn't get any support from him. But now seemed to be the right time to pay him a visit. I wanted to make sure I was not holding on to any unforgiveness and wanted him to acknowledge responsibility for what he did to me. He was surprised when I called him, requesting a meeting with him. He assumed I had aborted the baby since I never made another contact with him. I could tell he was very nervous about my showing up, twenty-five years later. But, he agreed to meet with me.

I was not sure about what I was doing, but I did seek some counsel with my pastor and other Christian friends. I had heard that it's hard to get forgiveness because the other person becomes so defensive that you never get complete forgiveness. I studied forgiveness and listened to tapes and lectures about it. It was something that I had to do. When he came in and sat down, he immediately started the conversation with an apology for the way he treated me that evening. He knew what he had done, and he knew that it was wrong. He asked me what I wanted from him. I lifted my arms out to him and said, I have carried this for twenty-five years. Here, you take it. Our son may show up on your doorstep. That seemed frightening to him. He married a few weeks after he last saw me, and they had a son who was born six months after Mac was born. He did not want his wife to know about this.

I didn't know anything about this man. So I asked him who his parents were, where he had lived, and some other small talk. He told me his mother lived close by where my mother lived and attended church. That prompted me to ask him about his relationship with God. He said he had no relationship with God. What popped into my head was strange, but I went with it and said, "Your mother has been praying for you for many years now. Go see her, and she'll help you get yourself right with God." He said, "Okay, I will."

Just last year, my granddaughter Lisa, Mac's daughter, called me, asking if I knew anything about the history of Mac's family. She was working on her son's DNA and wanted to know if she would find any strange diseases or happenings in his lineage. We googled his name, and immediately, his obituary popped up. He had died just a few months before, and all of his genealogy was spelled out, including the names of his spouse, parents, and two sons.

When I saw this, I was so glad I had forgiven that man. I felt freedom from all of the shame and guilt. For God to give me the courage to talk to him about getting right with Him, I gave thanks. I feel sure he did come to the saving knowledge of Jesus Christ as his Lord and Savior.

As I look back over all of these events, I realize God knew my heart, the heart of a birthmother. While I had buried the memories, He knew they needed to be unearthed so I could heal, and so my son, Mac, could also heal. I am thankful for God's amazing grace, and the love he displayed by reuniting me with my son. After all, God is a good Father, and He knows what it's like to love a child and to give them up for the good of others.

"Now to him who is able to do immeasurably more than all we ask or imagine, according to his power that is at work within us, to him be glory in the church and in Christ Jesus throughout all generations, forever and ever! (Ephesians 3:20–21).

Brenda Mahon is a local businesswoman who devotes her time and talents as a board member to a local non-profit Christian organization, Involved for Life, Inc. Involved for Life helps women and their families through their two Dallas area centers: Downtown Pregnancy Center and Uptown Women's Center. Contact Brenda at:
Brenda@uptownwomenscenter.com.

Thoughts to Ponder
from A Birth Mother's Secret

1. God hears the longings of our heart.

2. We can have no secrets from God.

3. Honesty in relationships provides restoration.

What secrets are you holding on to?

Would not God have discovered it, since he knows the secrets of the heart? — Psalm 44:21

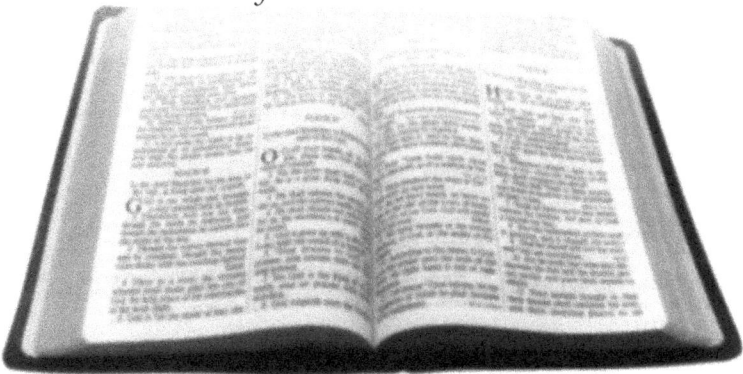

Explosions
by Sharon Hill

It was 9:12 a.m. on April 16 when a small Texas town suffered the worst industrial accident in the history of our nation. A father was drinking coffee from a green mug. His eleven-year-old son headed to school on his bicycle. The mother finished getting ready for work and was helping her four year-old daughter put on her patent leather shoes to go to her grandmother's house for the day.

All of a sudden there was a loud boom outside. The house shook.

The mother ran to the front door to look out. Within a few seconds, that same door fell on her, severely breaking her collarbone. The little girl rushed to look out of two large windows in the bedroom. At that very second, the window sill flew over her head, missing her by a few inches. Although she was sprayed with glass from the windows, she suffered only one small cut inside her lip. A miracle!

Texas City was a small town of 15,000 people, surrounded by chemical refineries along the coast of Texas, near Galveston. A French freighter, the Grand Camp, carrying ammonia nitrate fertilizer entered the ocean port, on fire, and exploded in the harbor near Monsanto Chemical Plant, only two miles from this family's home. This set off a chain reaction of explosions to two other chemical factories.

The Texas City Explosion is said to have had the force of an atomic bomb.

- 580 people were killed (including the entire Fire Department)
- One out of every three people were disabled or injured
- Every home was destroyed or badly damaged

The roof lifted off this family's small frame two-bedroom home and the house was picked up and turned on the foundation blocks. Their postman, who was delivering the neighbor mail, was blown to dust. The high school gymnasium converted to a morgue.

Riding her tricycle down the sidewalk just a few miles away, in a small town called La Marque, was another little girl. Her name was Kay Bailey, Former Senator Kay Bailey Hutchinson, the first woman to represent Texas in the United States Senate. That day, Kay also felt the ground shaking beneath her tricycle.

Pieces and chunks of the Grand Camp covered the city. When this family drove down the alley to leave town, a piece of the ship lodged in his car, puncturing a hole in the radiator. That caused them to stop many times to add water. Yes, in fact, that was my family. I was the little girl, and I still have a piece of the ship found in our front yard that terrible day.

Because of the many ambulances, fire trucks, emergency vehicles, and hundreds of people badly burned or injured, we could not get medical help for my mother, so we left town to drive to my grandmother's house in Aransas Pass, Texas.

Although we were posted on the city's Missing List, presumed dead, we were survivors of the Texas City Explosion and that was a day God had his hand on my life, and the lives of my family. It was a day I will never forget.

Can you think of a time in when God had His hand on your life?

Little did I know at the time there would be many more explosions in my life.

I met someone who left a huge impact on my life. I would go back to her words many times when the explosions of life tried to take me down.

Following the Texas City Explosion, We moved to another house in Texas City. A woman named Mrs. Frank lived across the street. Mrs. Frank and her family had been missionaries in India. Although I grew up in a church, we never carried our Bible to church, read the Bible in our home, or prayed as a family. But when I was six-years-old I would run across the street to visit Mrs. Frank. She would tell me about Jesus and pray for me. There were Bibles and many pictures of Jesus in the Frank's home. Even though I was just a little girl, I had a hunger to learn about God.

One night I had a dream. I dreamed I saw Jesus' head surrounded by a large cloud. When I awoke I could hardly wait to run across the street and tell Mrs. Frank.

"Mrs. Frank, I had a dream about Jesus. He was dressed in a white robe and surrounded by a cloud."

Mrs. Frank was pleased and continued to tell me more about God and His love for me. Then as time passed, I would have the same dream again. There He was, dressed in a white robe surrounded by a cloud. With excitement I would race across the street. "Mrs. Frank, Mrs. Frank. I had that dream about Jesus!" "Oh, Sharon," she would say. "Jesus loves you very much."

Over the next few months, I had the same dream several times and would always run as fast as my little legs would carry me to tell Mrs. Frank.

Then one night, I had the dream, but this time it was different. Jesus was there, surrounded by that cloud. I dreamed He stretched out His arm, draped in a white robe with long sleeves, and He moved His arm and hand to the right toward me. I raced across the street so fast I nearly broke my legs. I couldn't wait to tell Mrs. Frank about *this* dream.

"Oh, Sharon" Mrs. Frank said, "Jesus loves you very much and He is inviting you to Himself." And then Mrs. Frank said these words, "Sharon, you are specially chosen."

"Specially chosen."

Throughout my life, I often thought about that dream and Mrs. Frank's words. As I went through many deep valleys in the years that followed (as maybe you have too), I never forgot those four encouraging words:

"You are specially chosen."

And to my recollection, these were the first words of encouragement about Jesus, spoken into my life.

A few years later at a Christian Youth Camp, at age nine, I understood more about God's plan of salvation. I prayed to receive Christ into my life as my personal Savior. As I grew older, I understood that anything I think, do or say that breaks the heart of God is sin but when I confess my sins, those are taken care of on the cross and forgotten. I came to know and understand God's wonderful promise found in Psalm 138:8 (NKJ): "The Lord will perfect that which concerns me."

Growing up, I was fortunate my mother always took me to church but my father did not attend. He was an alcoholic, which brought me much pain and embarrassment. It was difficult to invite friends over because I did not know how my father would act.

However, my father loved me very much and I loved him. He called me his "princess." On occasion, I would talk to him about Jesus but I am not certain he ever surrendered his life to Him.

With on-and-off dysfunction at home, I wanted nothing more than to leave home and get married as soon I could. I wanted to have my own home, a Christian home, with no alcohol where I could bake bread, make curtains, and have babies.

Upon graduation from high school, I did just that. I married a Christian man who planned to complete college and attend seminary. Through my eyes, the candlelight wedding was second to Princess Kate's wedding, complete with a large performing choir and five hundred people attending. My father was able to give me away at the wedding and he was proud of his beautiful princess, adorned in a magnificent wedding dress.

My father later died at age 54 from a sudden heart attack. It was no coincidence that years later, I came across a small plaque with my name and title, Sharon PRINCESS. It reminded me of my father. The scripture inscribed on the plaque was John 15:16 (KJV): "I have chosen you." That was the message spoken by Mrs. Frank and I again claimed that promise for my life.

As our new life together began and continued, my husband ended up dropping out of college and having many different kinds of jobs. Life was very unstable. There were times we had little or no money. Then to my shock, my husband came home one day, on my birthday, to announce he was leaving me and our children for a woman we both knew. She was four months pregnant with his baby.

It was another explosion going off in my life. I was devastated. Yes, I was abandoned at the age of twenty-five with three small children. In agony, I cried out to God and screamed these words, "But Mrs. Frank, you said I was specially chosen!"

I didn't understand. *This doesn't happen to Christians*, I thought. *How could this happen to me, and my precious children?*

A few days later after many hours of tearful prayers and walking in disbelief, I found the strength to call my children around me (ages one, three, and five), and tell them their father would not be living with us anymore. I assured them we had God and His love, we had each other, and we would be just fine. To my surprise, my five-year-old son then asks me this question, "Mom, is it okay if I sit at the head of the table?" And that is exactly what he did.

I sought godly counsel and of course had Biblical grounds for divorce, but I certainly was embarrassed, as a Christian, to be a divorcee. It was like a mark on my forehead. At the time, we had been youth directors in our church for over two hundred teenagers. Humiliating.

The day came when my lawyer and I went to court. Seven years of marriage was over in about three minutes. As we walked out of the courthouse the lawyer said, "Well, Sharon, you are a free woman." A *free* woman? I didn't want to be a free woman. All I wanted was to have a Christian home, bake bread, make curtains, and have babies. I found myself walking alone around the courthouse calling out to God for peace and comfort in the midst of the most recent explosion. And I cannot explain how powerfully I felt His loving arms around me. As we read in the scriptures, I knew Jesus became my husband for this season of my life. I had a supernatural peace.

I spent many hours in God's Word and in prayer. By God's grace, I became stronger each day. I wrote my way to healing in a journal. I became a survivor and provider for my little family. I went on to work for a marketing company owned by Christian friends, and became a conference speaker. At age twenty-five I stood in front of thousands of distributors across the nation as a trainer and motivational speaker. I often shared my testimony about the love and grace of God. I knew that no matter what the people in the audience were experiencing I wanted to give a word of hope and encouragement by telling about what God had done in my life, regardless of the loss and circumstances.

I was single less than a year and remarried a man, who loved my children and adopted them. We all had the same last name; that was a huge thing to me. We moved into a beautiful home and had a fourth child, a beautiful daughter. Life was luxurious. I had live-in maids, we traveled as a couple and as a family, had a large hunting lease, enrolled our children in Christian schools, and were both very involved with our children activities and sports. We went on fishing trips, ski trips and wonderful vacations.

But following what began as a wonderful Cinderella story I found myself, five years later, living with a man who entertained his customers a lot and became an alcoholic. He was a man who, to my surprise, did not know Christ. In fact, he was an abusive alcoholic. As his addiction to alcohol spiraled out of control, my children suffered from the abuse and emotional pain of a dysfunctional home. Oh, you might have read about us in the society column of the newspaper but behind closed doors, life was worse than words can express.

Everyone handles pain in different ways. How about you? Have you ever coped with depression by overeating, overusing prescription drugs, alcohol, or other drugs and mind changing chemicals? God can help you through your pain.

I suffered the most severe pain a mother can ever experience. Because of the abuse and dysfunction, some of my teenagers began using drugs and alcohol to mask their pain. They began making poor choices, resulting in serious consequences. One son was incarcerated many times for DUI's.

After twelve years of marriage, and for our own safety, I was forced to leave husband #2 and file for divorce. Although I again had Biblical grounds for the split, I experienced embarrassment as a Christian, devastation, and severe heartache. It was another explosion, leaving my life in rubble.

I would often think of Mrs. Frank and those words she spoke into my life years earlier. "You are specially chosen."

And this time, somehow in my spirit, despite the wreckage around me, I knew I was. You see, Mrs. Frank left words of encouragement that became a lifeline.

God began to rebuild my life after this when I launched a successful career as President of an international marketing company with over three thousand women. The success of this company brought recognition on television, radio, magazine, newspapers, and presentations, including one to the White House staff and wives of Senators on Capitol Hill. My company was formed and operated back in the 1980's. Although I was President and responsible for the success, products and sales of the company, it was owned by a holding company who held the purse strings. Unfortunately, when the oil crash hit the economy, my company suffered cash flow problems and came to an end.

Although I lived in a large home with a Cadillac in the driveway, I was without title and a job. I was over qualified for jobs or they underpaid. With two hundred people every day walking out of their houses and over 20,000 foreclosures in the Houston area, I could not sell my home. I soon spent my savings to survive and became almost penniless. I did get a job but the pay was not much. I spent two years in what I call the desert. Those were the days God didn't say yes or no. It seemed like he didn't say anything at all on what I should do next. Have you ever had that experience?

I fasted and prayed a lot. I grew leaps and bounds spiritually. Many times, God pulls out treasures from the wreckage.

One day I was invited to a friend's home in the Dallas/Fort Worth area to hear a speaker. Across the room, I eyed the best looking man I had ever seen in my life. Ronnie Hill. He had received Christ just five days earlier. He was almost forty-years-old and had never married. I was a grandmother. To bring our lives together, there was a lot of work to do, but God can do all things. We dated long distance for twenty months, and were married in the same living room where we met. This was indeed one of God's miracles, all part of His perfect timetable. God knew I needed a "gentle" man, and that is what I received when He gave me Ronnie. The Scripture that best tells our story is found in Job 42:12 (KJV): "So the Lord blessed the latter end of Job (Sharon & Ronnie) more than the beginning."

Recently, I came across another scripture in the Living Bible that jumped right off the page, and best tells my entire story: "For I have specially chosen you, said the Lord Almighty" (Haggai 2:23 TLB).

I could not believe my eyes! Those were the exact words Mrs. Frank spoke over my life as a small child. I cherished that verse from that point on.

Many people ask how I survived these life explosions, full of pain and trauma. The answer is I learned about the power of prayer and journaling. I learned to write my way to healing and how to hear from God on paper. That led me to author the *OnCall Prayer Journal.*

I've also learned there will always be explosions in life, some larger than others. About three years ago, due to circumstances, my alcoholic son became homeless. He lived and slept under a bush in a vacant lot in the frigid cold weather for six months. The pain in my heart was so intense I could hardly breathe or function. That was when God said to me, "Sharon, you have been praying all these years that your son be delivered from alcohol. Your son drinks to mask pain. This is how I want you to pray for him: "Pray that he will feel my love; "to grasp how wide and long and high and deep is the love of Christ, and to know this love that

154

surpasses knowledge—that he may be filled to the measure of all the fullness of God" (Eph. 3:18-19).

And next I want you to pray these five steps:

1) The scales will fall from his eyes (Acts 9:18).
2) For total surrender (Joshua 22:5).
3) God would remove the heart of stone and give him a new heart (Ezekiel 36:26).
4) He will have a hunger for God's Word (Deuteronomy 4:29).
5) He will become a mighty man of God (Zechariah 10:7 and Psalm 112:1-2).

With that Word from God, I then prayed this prayer: "Lord, you gave me Your Son, and now I give you mine."

Today God is doing a great work in my son's life.

Everyone has a story. Everyone has their own explosions that detonate in their lives. Maybe you can relate to some of mine. Like me, we don't always understand why some things happen or why we suffer pain. God does not promise us a life without problems. But He does promise us He will carry us through the pain. He carried me through devastation many times. And He will carry you out of the wreckage. God says, He will never leave you or forsake you. He certainly never left me.

I know I am specially chosen. You are too.

Sharon Hill is the Founder of OnCall Prayer, Inc. She is also President of Fellowship of Professional Women and the Executive Director for Christian Women in Media Association. Sharon is the author of the OnCall Prayer Journal and The Power of Three-How a Protective Shield of Intentional Prayer Can Transform Your Life.
www.OnCallPrayer.org

Thoughts to Ponder
from Explosions

1. Explosions will come in your life, but God can diffuse any explosive.

2. Be prepared by having "Living Water" nearby.

3. God can rebuild from the rubble.

What area of your life needs to be restored by God?

For the eyes of the Lord are on the righteous and his ears are attentive to their prayer. — 1 Peter 3:12

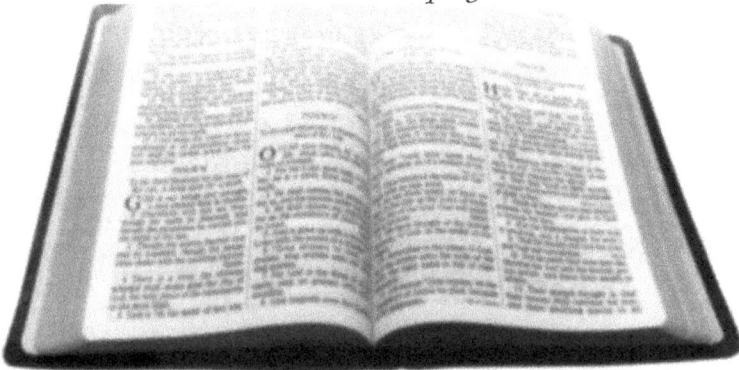

Flashes in the Fog

by Arlener Poydras

Have you ever been in the dark? I mean really in the dark where you can't see your own hand in front of your face. When we are in our darkest moments, even the slightest bit of light catches our attention and lights our pathway. Regardless of our position in life, our financial status, or even our religious belief, darkness does not discriminate. Darkness is darkness, pain is pain, sickness is sickness, and sorrow is sorrow. However, God has a way of sending flashes of unexpected light into the darkest of foggy places.

It was a warm February afternoon in 2012, around lunchtime, when I looked at my husband and said, "I need a glass of wine." He gazed at me and said, "I could use a drink myself." You see, my only biological child, my son AJ, passed away on February 20, 2012 and I was looking for relief in all the wrong places. So my husband drove over thirty-five miles to a liquor store in another city, in a part of town where we thought no one would see the preacher and his wife. Upon arrival, there was only one car in the parking lot. As we parked, I saw an elderly gentleman with gray hair getting out of his car. I remember admiring his car, and thinking to myself, "What a beautiful baby blue Mercedes convertible, and it's a perfect day for it!"

After my husband went into the store, he emerged a few minutes later with an odd look on his face, holding a bag at arm's length in front of him. When he got into the car he said, "You are not going to believe what happened." I thought the store had been robbed or something. As my husband backed out of the parking space, the elderly man came out of the door. As we passed in front him on the parking lot, my husband lowered the car window on my side and pointed toward the man and said, "That man paid for all of our stuff!" The man looked up and slowly walked toward our car. My hand was on the door of the car, the elderly gentleman then placed his hand on top of my hand and said, "God told me to tell you, He knows what he is doing, and it's going to be alright." I looked into his crystal blue eyes, and it felt like I was looking through them into heaven. He was smiling as tears rolled down my face. He squeezed my hand, said "God bless you" and walked away. My husband and I drove home in silence. Needless to say, the preacher and his wife did not have that glass of wine.

God knows where you are, and His love for you will stalk you, even if you try to hide in a liquor store in another town. I believe the man in the parking lot was a messenger from God. He was sent to give hope to grieving parents who were roaming around in the fog looking for something to ease their pain. He brought a little of God's light to us in a moment of darkness. I call these unexpected encounters with God, "Flashes in the Fog." Just when you are about to give up or you can't take one more thing, God makes himself known to you in unexpected ways. Don't miss Him in the small things; look for Him, expect Him and wait for Him.

My journey with God started years ago and I did not even realize how involved God was in the details of my life. As a little girl, my grandmother took us to a small traditional church where we were part of the children's choir. One evening, my brothers and I forgot that granny was going to pick us up for choir rehearsal. We were dressed in play clothes, shorts and sneakers. When granny stopped by to pick us up for rehearsal, we simply hopped in the car without thinking. After choir rehearsal I heard my granny talking loudly with another lady dressed in all white. The other lady was saying we could not come back because I wore shorts to church and it was inappropriate. I did not ask my grandmother about the conversation, but the experience incorrectly shaped my view of God. I grew up believing that I had to "dress" a certain way or "perform" a certain way, or "not do certain things" or Jesus would not love me anymore.

Shortly after that experience my favorite uncle was murdered. During that time, I remember being in the back seat of my parent's car, saying to Jesus, "If you are real, help me stop crying," and He did. From then on I believed Jesus was real. I did not understand everything, but I accepted Jesus on faith.

However, in the back of my mind and heart, I still believed I had to perform in order to be accepted by God. As the second oldest of nine children, I did everything. I cleaned house, changed diapers, was employed at age fifteen, maintained straight A's in school and worked hard to meet the approval of others. Finally, at age 19, I found out some good news! Jesus already completed the performance. I did not have to do everything perfectly, or solve every problem to be loved by Him. I was one tired little girl. I needed to accept that Jesus paid the price for my inability to get everything right. Now that I really understood with my head, as well as my heart, I decided to get baptized again as an adult. For the first time in my life I felt free. I did not have to perform anymore for the approval of people or God.

But old habits die hard. I knew I did not have to perform to be accepted by Jesus, but I still depended on myself to get things done. I graduated from college, married my high school sweetheart, and had a son. While married, I completed an MBA and CPA, and adopted a nine-month-old little girl. I was Superwoman! However, I felt it was all me; *my* effort, *my* smarts and *my* plan. My life was bright and sunny. I know God was there with me since that day in the back seat of my parent's car, but my life was so bright that I missed Him.

By age 30, everything started to crumble. I found out the MBA stood for "Married but Alone." I ended up divorced with a two small children. After trying to hold it together financially for a while, I knew I needed to make a tough decision. With two children and one income, I could not make ends meet. It was a dark time in my life. I made a decision to go home to my mother and start over.

When I went to church that Sunday I thought, *Since I don't have enough money to pay my bills anyway, I might as well tithe for the first time.* This was going to be a new beginning, the right way. On Monday morning I called my landlord to tell him I was moving out, and he asked why. I explained I could not afford to stay any longer. He said I was a good tenant, lowered my monthly payment by $200, and waived my late fees. How did he know how much I was short? How did he know he gave me back more than double what I gave as a tithe on Sunday?

There was a light in the darkness, hope for my distress. I began to realize God provided all of the goodness in my life, and even though I didn't notice him, he was always there. However when things were dark, I saw him much more clearly.

I came to the end of myself and walked into an intimate, amazing, indescribably delicious relationship with the God of the universe. This experience began a twenty-year journey of moving from knowing about God from afar, to getting to know Jesus up close and personal. This intimate love relationship came by reading his Word, prayer, Bible study, attending church, and serving his people. Previously, I did not have a relationship with God, I just knew about him, and I believed in Him.

I grew closer to God by talking to him about everything: good times, bad times, mundane times, just all of the time. I loved God and his people and I wanted them to love Him the way I did. So I began serving God's people and teaching them his Word. There were ups and downs, mistakes and successes, faith and doubt, but a close relationship developed. A close relationship with Jesus is the most gratifying, amazing, unexplainable relationship in the world.

However, a close relationship does not exempt us from trouble. I know that death is part of life, and I have had my share of people pass away, friends, family, my granny, and my dad. In November, 2011 my youngest sister died. My son, AJ, my husband and I were next to her bedside at a local hospital. After she took her last breath, there was a peace that came over her and us. I pulled out my phone and pulled up the song, "Trust in Jesus" by Third Day. When we pulled the curtain back in the Emergency Room, the staff was rocking along with us.

It was beautiful.

One hundred days later, on Feb 20, 2012, the phone rang around 9:00 a.m. I missed the call but returned the call immediately because the phone number was from Abilene, Texas. My son, AJ, moved to Abilene in November, 2011. The police officer on the other end of the phone told me my son was no longer with us. My need for God escalated exponentially at that moment. As people began gathering at our home, it was simply unbelievable. My pastor came over, and before he left, wanted to pray with us. Immediately after he finished praying, a song started to play on the intercom, "Trust in Jesus" by Third Day. My husband and I looked at each other with tears in our eyes. That still small voice inside of me quietly said, "If I am good enough for your sister, I am good enough for your only son."

This did not look or feel like my Savior, Jesus, my friend Jesus, my "everything" Jesus. This felt like Jesus no longer loved me. I felt betrayed. I felt like the gospel was not true. God was not good. I was appalled, terrorized and taunted by death. In my anguish I even yelled at God. In his mercy and compassion, He did not yell back! I was like a child having a temper tantrum when her favorite toy is taken away. God grabbed me as I kicked, flailing my arms, shaking my head and screaming; He put me in a vice grip called love until a protective fog settled over my life.

Over the next week, God clouded my mind and my emotions in an amazing way. So much so He enabled me to bury my baby, do an appeal to those who attended the funeral, who were not believers in Jesus. I used the song "Trust in Jesus," to comfort others, and I did not shed a tear. I recognized God in the midst of my grief, holding me up for His glory. There were many people at the funeral that loved and knew me, but were not believers in Jesus Christ. I loved these people; many were coworkers for over twenty years and were some of the nicest, smartest, and honest people I ever knew. I desperately wanted them to know God was holding me up. I had nothing to do with it.

In the weeks after the funeral I received many inquiries about this Jesus that I believe in. How was I able to stand on that day, what was the meaning of the Scriptures that were read during the funeral, and on and on and on. I was grateful to share Christ during this season.

What has terrorized or hurt you beyond your wildest nightmare? What did you do? What did God do?

God will use bad things to send us deeper into his word and into a tangible and intimate relationship with him.

When God removed the fog and the cold, harsh reality settled in that AJ was not coming back. I began the journey of grief that felt like walking naked in subzero weather on broken glass. That's when I found myself at a liquor store looking for relief. After God made himself known through a stranger, I totally surrendered again.

162

But this would be another level of closeness with my God. When we got home from the liquor store, I went into my bedroom, closed the door, entered my bathroom, closed the door, then went into my closet, and closed the door. I lay on the floor for hours. I prayed to God, saying, "I can't do it. If you don't rescue me, I will just die on the closet floor, and I am okay with that. For weeks on end I would go there and yell and cry and earnestly talk with God about my misery and grief. God did not say a word, but I knew he was there. He knew I could not hear him through the pain and darkness. God knows us, he knows our personalities, and he deals with each of us differently.

In my mind, I was certain of who God said He was in his Word, and I wanted it to be true in my heart again. Burying my only biological child did not look like the God I knew but God showed me He was the same God, at age six, at age nineteen, when I got married, divorced, and even now. God began to show me His character by showing up in his creation at just the right moments.

One morning, during one of my temper tantrums, I was thumbing through an old Bible and saw my name and the date April 9, 2009 written by Psalm 116. I realized it was my grandmother's name, Arlener, and the date of her funeral next to her favorite verse. Psalm 116:1. She always recited verse 1: "I love the Lord for he heard my voice; he heard my cry for mercy." God whispered, "Keep reading" and I did. So I read the entire passage and it spoke completely to my anguish and grief. This became my favorite Psalm. During my lunch hour, I walked around the lake at my office, repeating this Psalm until I had it memorized. The Scripture spoke to all of my pain points and became true to me verse-by-verse.

Going through my son's things one day, I fell to the floor as a wave of grief came in. I was just about to go into tantrum mode when a text message came in from a friend that I talk with twice a year. It said, "I bind depression right now in the name of Jesus." I immediately looked around because I wondered who was watching me. How did they know? God was on the floor with me and sent me a simple message: "Not today; no tantrums today." I got up and started cleaning AJ's room.

In September of that year I took a week off to pack up AJ's things. It was a difficult week. My daughter and I went to church the following Sunday with heavy hearts.

Chris, a brilliant young man who is autistic, attends our church. He has a special thing he does with birthdays. If you tell him your birthday and year, he tells you, within seconds, what day of the week you were born. He can also tell if there was a storm or any other significant event on that day. So he came up to me and my daughter, yelling with his unique stutter, "Sis Poydras, Sis Poydras, I have been thinking about AJ a lot this week. I miss him." I got choked up and said, "Me too, Chris." He looked at us and said, "Oh well, that's okay. He is in heaven" and abruptly walked away. My daughter and I started laughing and said, "Amen Chris."

A few weeks later, I had a couple of visitors with me. Chris walked up and asked them if they were left-handed or right-handed? They looked at each other and answered. Chris then told the visitors that AJ was also left-handed. Then Chris immediately corrected himself and said, "Oh, he's is in heaven now, so he writes with both hands." Then he abruptly walked away. Chris runs with the angels. He delivered a powerful message to me not once, but twice. I was not hearing God speak to me, so he sent Chris my way, and I was grateful.

In spite of my sin, in spite of my anger, in spite of my faithlessness, in spite of questions, my lack of obedience, God was gracious to me and showed up in a ways that I would notice and say that he loves me still. He will meet us anywhere, even in a liquor store to let us know that he loves us and He knows what He is doing.

There is no darkness with God. Look for the "Flashes in the Fog" in every stage of your life. They will make you smile through tears and worship God in spite of the darkness.

Arlener's mantra is, "Jesus is my everything and my enough!" She is the author of the book Flashes in the Fog. She is President of The Artis-the-Artist Foundation and serves with the "Meet Me at the Cross" (MM@TC!) Prayer Ministry. She is married to Minister L.A. Poydras, and has a daughter, Marie. www.Artis-the-Artist.com

Thoughts to Ponder
from Flashes in the Fog

1. God's light can penetrate any darkness.

2. Performance has nothing to do with acceptance; God accepts us just as we are.

3. God provides encouragement in unexpected places.

> **How has someone's encouragement made a difference in your faith journey?**

Have I not commanded you? Be strong and courageous. Do not be afraid; do not be discouraged, for the Lord your God will be with you wherever you go. — Joshua 1:9

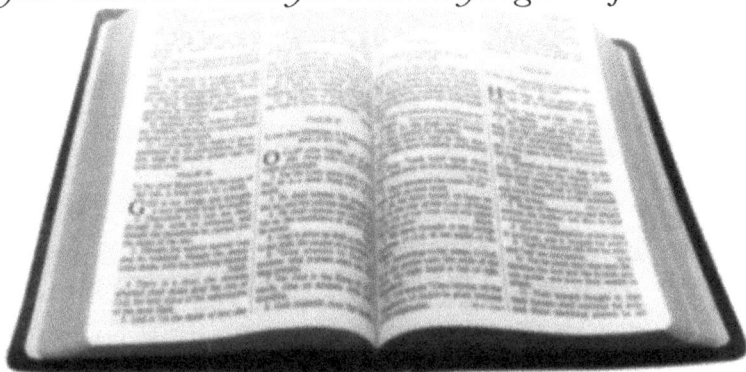

The Fixer

by Janet Scholl

Why couldn't I fix this?

I was smart. I was young. I was healthy. I was married with three beautiful girls.

It looked like I had it all, but I was beaten down, afraid and embarrassed. No one knew. No one even suspected, and why would they? I was very good at pretending.

Growing up, life was simple and good. I knew I was loved and didn't really have anything to worry about. I spent my time at the dinner table, on the tennis court or in the church. I don't remember ever not being in church. Even when we couldn't go, we had a service at home. I memorized verses, learned how to recite the books of the Bible, listened to stories about giants, whales, bad guys and good guys. I knew the characters and could sing all the Vacation Bible School songs. I knew Jesus. He was God's Son. He was the good guy in the Bible, and I colored beautiful pictures of Him.

When I was ten years old, with a childlike faith, I stood in front of the church and told everyone I believed Jesus was the Son of God, and was later baptized. I didn't hear the angels sing or have an emotional reaction. It was just a simple act of obeying what the Bible told me to do. So life resumed as normal. I continued going to church and believing in Jesus, but to say I had a profound understanding of the Lord's almighty power would be like suggesting an ant has a profound understanding of the power of the worldwide web. I believed, and that was enough for now.

My dad was a highly respected tennis coach. I learned how to work hard, on and off the court. I was not only taught how to play tennis, I was also taught values. I was confident, strong and blessed with a natural talent. I worked hard to win state and national championships. I played a pro-am tour in Europe, and I was on my way to play in a college tournament in Hawaii when I was diverted.

I never made it to the college tournament because I met someone at the Campus Christian Center. On the surface, he looked perfect. He went to church three times a week, made me laugh, and he wanted to get married. It seemed to make sense. My mother was only nineteen when she married; most of the women in my family married at a very early age and it worked out for all of them. Sure, let's get married! I can truly say I don't remember giving a single thought to praying about this decision. I just did it. So we married in the church, surrounded by family.

Then my picture-perfect life changed for the worse. My new husband's anger appeared almost overnight. He pushed me into walls. The anger and the level of abuse quickly escalated into much more, and it never stopped for thirteen years.

I was overwhelmed and exhausted. I could hide the physical wounds, but the emotional wounds left deep scars. I lost my confidence and was afraid. But no one had to know. I could fix this if I just did the right things, trying harder, working harder.

I was struggling endlessly to make everything perfect, trying to please my husband, convincing everyone I was happy, attempting to control every situation. I was walking on eggshells, and things kept getting worse.

I often thought about how easy it would be to sit in a running car in my garage, but I couldn't do that to my babies. Maybe a truck would hit me.

Suicidal thoughts came because I was tired. Eleven years into the marriage, I exhausted everything I knew to try. I was beaten and could not "fix it." One day I found myself in our family doctor's office without an appointment. I walked in and asked to see the doctor. I broke down, begging him to stop prescribing medication for my husband. "If you knew how much alcohol he was consuming you wouldn't prescribe him all those pills," I said.

The doctor realized there was a more immediate problem. Me. He directed me down the hall to a counselor. I didn't even take the time to stop and think about what I was doing. I just followed his advice and walked down the hall, again entering a doctor's office without an appointment. A wonderful counselor and a true gentleman greeted me.

The counselor listened and counseled me for two years. He reminded me of the Serenity Prayer. I knew that prayer because it hung in my grandmother's home. It said to accept the things I could not change, to ask for courage to change the things I could, and wisdom to know the difference. I finally had peace in leaving my abusive marriage. I gave everything I had to give.

It was time to make the call to my parents. I knew if I told them what was happening, they would rescue me, and they did. That's one of the reasons I never told them sooner. I wasn't ready to give up, and I didn't want to explain why I was choosing to stay. But now I had made the call, and my daddy arrived like a knight in shining armor. I was barely able to move; I just went through the motions, packed what we needed and loaded it into the car.

I'll never forget the moment I looked in the rearview mirror from the backseat and saw my daddy crying. I couldn't remember ever seeing him cry before. I felt horrible. This is what I feared. I didn't want to hurt people. But it was done. I had to press on.

People ask me why I didn't tell anyone; why I didn't leave. I still can't explain it. There's not a simple answer to that question. A little over a year after we married, we gave birth to our first daughter prematurely. She was tiny. When you've shared an experience like this, it complicates life even more and you hold on to what you know. But after thirteen years I had to let go.

Since I hadn't talked with anyone but God for the first eleven years of my marriage, we developed a very close relationship. Jesus was no longer just a character in a Bible story like I learned as a child; He was my friend and my comforter. He was the one who sustained me. It wasn't just about book knowledge anymore; I gained heart knowledge.

Now it was time to start a new, easier life. I paid my dues; I'd met my quota of pain and I survived.

While the next four years were challenging, I still saw myself heading back up the mountaintop. I was rebuilding my life and my confidence.

A single mom of three little girls, with a full-time job, I volunteered as a volleyball coach for the older girls' teams. I had the love and support of my family and friends, and my faith was stronger than ever. Life wasn't easy, but it was good.

One day, I heard someone say "Hi Shorty." Since I'm six feet tall, I had never been called that in my life. It got my attention. I turned around and found myself looking at a tall, handsome stranger. It was love at first sight for me! But this time I wasn't going to rush into anything. I had to take care of my girls. Of course he wasn't too anxious to rush into anything either. He needed to figure it out, because I was a package deal. We dated for four years before marrying, and I can truly say he is my Prince Charming. God blessed me with more than I could have ever imagined in a husband. I don't know how I would have made it through the following years without him.

My youngest was one-and-a-half years old when my first marriage ended. As the years progressed, people told me they were concerned she wasn't developing at the pace of her peers. I was in complete denial. I enrolled her in kindergarten, and soon received a call they wanted to meet with me. The next journey began. Years of testing, years of therapies, doctor after doctor, a laundry list of diagnoses. Every time another doctor would add a new diagnosis, I grieved all over again. One day, a very wise person told me, "She's the same child she was before you walked into that doctor's office; it's just a new label." That was true, and it helped tremendously, but she had so many labels.

At the same this was going on, my middle daughter was complaining her back hurt. We went to doctors, specialists, and more doctors. She had X-rays, MRI's, CT Scans, and every test imaginable. With each doctor came a new diagnosis and a new treatment plan, seven in all. She literally crawled through the house some days. Finally, after two years, we were convinced to try one more specialist. He ordered a full-body scan that revealed a stress fracture. A full body cast and a few months later, she was feeling no pain and feeling good, and I was again feeling like I could "fix things." At least I could find the doctors who could fix things, even if it did take a long time.

One day in the midst of all this, I called my parents to tell them the latest development in my seemingly never-ending list of medical updates. Daddy listened, then in his Texas drawl, with a little chuckle, he commented, "Well, after this, there'll be something else." What? Really? Where was the sympathy? Where was the encouragement? Hadn't I paid my dues and had my share of hard times?

But by now, I knew he was right. There's always another challenge in life. We aren't allotted one or two problems; in fact, there's no limit. Trials are a part of life, and I don't even get to choose the ones I want to experience. If I did, I would make sure they didn't involve my children suffering. I could take anything, but leave my girls alone!

A couple of months after my middle daughter's recovery from the back fracture, she came in one Saturday morning with a strange look on her face. She thought she was having seizures in her sleep. It didn't seem possible, but something about the look on her face told me I needed to take this serious. We started with a new set of doctors. At one point, I went to twenty-one doctors with Amy and Cara in less than two months. New tests, new X-rays, CT scans and MRI's. I don't know why, but I didn't expect the phone call so soon. They found something. I couldn't even pronounce that word the doctor just said, but I heard "brain surgeon." It was surreal. We scheduled an appointment with a world-famous surgeon and made the decision to let her go to the volleyball camp she had her heart set on. Can you imagine? How do you send your child off to a volleyball camp when she may need brain surgery? I still don't know how I let go of her for that week.

Amy went to Abilene Christian University for a weeklong camp, not knowing what would happen when she returned. I fasted and prayed. On the last night of her camp, my husband and I attended a service at our church. We prayed and we sang. I was overwhelmed with a sense of peace when we ended the evening with the song, "It is Well with My Soul." The words got my attention, "Whatever my lot, thou has taught me to say, it is well, it is well with my soul." Did I really believe that? Yes, I did. I gave the burden to God and He took away the immense feelings of fear and replaced it with peace.

As I walked out of the church, Amy called me. She was excited to tell me about the devotional they just had at camp. They had learned the story of the song "It is Well with My Soul."

Wow!

God used the same song to minister to both of us at the same time in two different cities. I knew, that I knew, that I knew, God was in control and everything was going to be okay.

When Amy came home from camp, we went to see the brain surgeon and scheduled the surgery. I was brave and confident in the One that could fix this, but I'll never forget the moment I saw her after surgery. She had thirty-two metal staples across the top of her head, and her golden blonde curls were matted with blood. All the tubes and monitors were overwhelming to look at. As a matter of fact, my daddy, my knight in shining armor, had to run out of the room. It was more than he could bear, but God filled me up with a strength I couldn't have had on my own. She spent a month in the hospital, and I was with her every moment.

Two months later, Amy was back in school getting ready for one of her senior dances. I was proud to be her mom. And secretly, I was a little proud of myself. I had "fixed this" by taking her to all the doctors, finding the best surgeon and nurturing her back to health.

Back to my youngest daughter. So far we had spent seven years trying to help her. Seven years of therapies, medications, research, and many tears. There were tears of exhaustion and frustration.

Why couldn't I "fix this?"

We hired an advocate to help us maneuver the school system. She was an absolute angel in my eyes. With direction and help, we found the answer.

Autism.

It didn't change Cara, but it helped us to understand why she acted the way she did, why she wasn't progressing the way she should, and it gave me a new hope that I could "fix" this too. I just needed to learn more, spend more money and try harder. More therapies, special diets, research, tutoring, Autism conferences, workshops, more reading, and more prayer. I prayed earnestly for healing. I wanted healing and I wanted answers. The more I read, the more I was convinced I knew the answer to "why," but all the answer did was make me angry. I was angry with everyone, doctors, teachers, pharmaceutical companies, the government, and myself. Anger was making me physically ill. It felt like I had a vice tightening on my temples.

One morning, I thought I clearly heard the message that I should forget the past and press on. It wasn't audible, but it just suddenly came to mind. I knew that scripture. I would have to look it up.

A couple mornings later, I was going through the motions, putting my makeup on, trying to get ready to face another day. I was depressed, and exhausted. At that time, I rarely listened to music while getting ready, but that particular morning, I needed anything inspirational. I turned on the radio and heard a song I had never heard before. The main theme of the song was about finding the strength through Jesus to press on.

Wait a minute, that's the scripture I just looked up, Philippians 3:13-14.

"Brothers and sisters, I do not consider myself yet to have taken hold of it. But one thing I do: Forgetting what is behind and straining toward what is ahead, I press on toward the goal to win the prize for which God has called me heavenward in Christ Jesus."

I did not hear the name of the song or the group, but I knew I had to find it! I went to the Christian bookstore that day and there it was. That song was my battle cry. I wore out the CD, and I'm sure I got more than a few weird looks while driving and singing my heart out with tears streaming down my face, but I didn't care. I was being restored again.

174

I drove home one evening, listening to my song, singing loudly and feeling stronger than I had in a long time. As I was driving, it occurred to me that my head didn't hurt. I couldn't remember the last time my head didn't hurt; but it was true, the pain and the intense pressure was gone.

Part of "pressing on" was the realization Cara needed more than we could give her. It was evident she needed to be in a group home; but if you've ever tried to find that needle in a haystack, you know it's not that easy. There are over 84,000 people in the greater Dallas Metroplex with intellectual and developmental disabilities who are unable to live independently, but only 2,000 beds. Many of these individuals will end up homeless when their parents die.

I knew my family wouldn't let that happen to Cara, but I didn't want to burden anyone. I was going to fix it. I would find a safe, clean, affordable place for Cara. I had a plan. God must have laughed because every time I tried to get Cara into the home I chose for her; inevitably, something unimaginable would happen and the door would close. What would we do? Waiting lists were long, and the private facilities I found cost as much as $4,500 per month. That wasn't even an option for us.

Once again, I found out God does his best work when we get out of the way. Sometimes we don't get out of the way willingly, so He has to move us out of the way. That's exactly what happened in our case. He moved us completely out of the way in circumstances I could never have imagined. Without a single doubt in our minds, we know Cara is exactly where God wants her because there's no other explanation for how everything transpired.

She is now living in a group home, one mile from my parents' home and five minutes from my oldest daughter's work. We know Cara will thrive and be happier living in this type of setting, but that hasn't made it easy. As a mom, I selfishly wanted to always take care of her, protect her, spoil her, and, when the time was right, I wanted to be the one to help her move in to her home, share the fun of seeing her make new friends and realize how much fun she's going to have, but that wasn't God's plan.

I think I got a taste of how Moses must have felt. He led the people to the Promised Land, but didn't get the privilege of seeing them enjoy it. Remember, I had been moved completely out of the way, I didn't get to help her move in, meet her roommates or decorate her room. I had to accept by faith that she would be okay. More than that, I had to decide God would always take care of her.

There was now peace about Cara, but in the midst of trying to fix my younger daughters, my oldest daughter had been suffering in silence. The counselor couldn't give me details, but wanted to tell me she should be on suicide watch. I was knocked off my feet.

What happened? I knew she was struggling. The relationship with her boyfriend and the relationship with her biological father were both bad, but was it something else? Was it me? Doctor/patient confidentiality kept him from telling me anything. He said it would all come out and he just needed to make sure I kept a close eye on her over the weekend.

I hung up. A horrible thought entered my mind. Did someone hurt her? Did he? I knew. I called her and asked the question I didn't want to hear the answer to.

Silence.

The silence spoke volumes. I was right. I had hurt before. I had hurt physically, mentally and emotionally, but my heart had never felt pain and sorrow like this. I literally fell to my knees in desperation.

I knew I couldn't fix this. I was powerless.

All I could do was pray, and I did. I prayed like I had never prayed before. So many times I gave my children to God, trusting He would take care of them; but then I always took them back again, relying on my ability to fix things. This time I knew only God could restore her.

It was a painful time, but we survived. At least I thought we were okay. A few years later, Jennifer hit bottom. She was beaten, tired, scarred, and crying out for help. She needed to leave her husband and move home with our grandson. My bad habit of thinking I could fix things showed up again. I was wrong. The harder I tried, the worse things got. Once again, I was in denial. But over time, I had to face the truth when the truth stared me in the face. There were lots of bottles of prescription pain pills, evidence of an addiction. It was time for me to let go again. I had to admit I was just as powerless over the drugs as my daughter was. I could not control her decisions or her actions. I felt guilty. I felt like a failure as a mom. We took her to a hospital for help. I was numb, but anything with the word "hope" gave me reason to press on. I went to sessions with her. I needed to learn what we were dealing with and how I could help. I learned I could not fix her problems, but it was enough right now just to stand by her, offer a hug and a shoulder for her to cry on. I learned I didn't cause it, I couldn't control it and I couldn't cure it. I had to give her up *again*. I'm a slow learner.

She made it through the thirty days. Now she's made it two years. I am so proud of her.

I believe with all my heart God has a purpose for our sufferings, and I believe Jennifer and Amy will do amazing things to help others. Even with Cara, I have people come up to me and show me simple messages of hope and encouragement she's written them on church attendance cards. My girls are beautiful shining stars in God's universe.

I am thankful God gave us the resources, knowledge, wisdom and abilities to fight for Cara's rights and safety, and to help Jennifer and Amy. I am a better person for all the trials and tribulations we endured. I wouldn't have chosen the journey, but I can honestly say I'm thankful for it. A very wise lady once told me we should pray that God would give our children enough pain to keep them on their knees. That's a hard prayer to pray, but it's true.

Like my daddy said, there'll always be another challenge, but I won't give up and I'm learning all the way. I've learned God doesn't just sustain me during adversity; He restores me. I've learned God doesn't waste adversity; He uses it. I trust He is doing something much larger with my life than merely giving me a good life, free of struggle, and I've learned to accept I don't have to know all the answers.

I have learned we will hurt, we will suffer, we will be treated unfairly, we will be taken advantage of, we will be betrayed, and we will experience disappointments. We will even experience these things from our own husbands, children, friends and family.

All the trials, all the struggles, all the suffering, all the worries, all the pain, all the unanswered questions, it's not about me and what I want, it's all part of God's story, and He can fix anything!

Janet Scholl was born and raised in Texas. Her Texas roots, Christian heritage and love for family run deep. She is married to her Prince Charming, has three daughters and four precious grandchildren. Janet's personal experiences through many trials and her will to press on, will encourage and challenge you.

Thoughts to Ponder
from The Fixer

1. There are some problems only God can fix.

2. God will give us situations outside of our control so we are forced to depend on Him.

3. No matter what life tosses at you, God will equip you.

How has God been your crisis manager?

Trust in the Lord with all your heart and lean not on your own understanding; in all your ways submit to him, and he will make your paths straight. — Proverbs 3:5–6

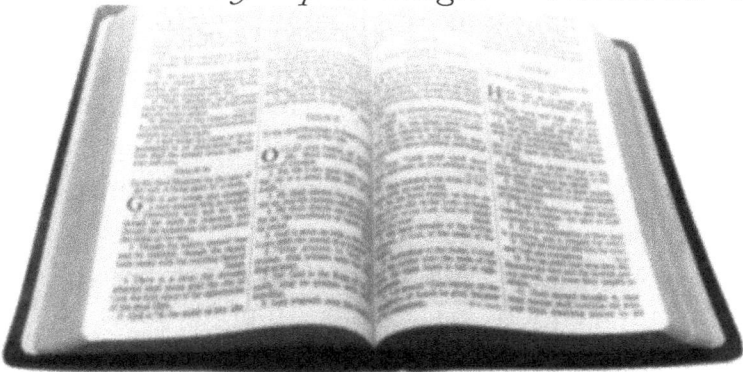

Why Ask Why?

by Carmyn Sparks

Have you noticed that one of the most painful questions people ask is: "Why did this happen to me?" Perhaps I can answer that question.

The human mind is interested in "why" more than anything else. As a child begins to communicate, they have more "why" questions than others can answer. "Why do birds fly? Why do you cry when you cut onions? Why do we blink? Why, why, why?

As children grow older the "why" becomes more self-centered, "Why can't I go?" "Why can't I have a car?" "Why do I have to go to school?"

Finally, as adulthood approaches, the why becomes "Why am I here?"

Some seek the answer their entire life and, sadly, never find the answer.

My name, Carmyn, is spelled with a "Y" instead of the usual spelling with an "E."

I've been called Cameron, Carolyn, Carmie, and the worst, Crayon!

Actually, no one knows why or how my father chose that name, and especially the "Y" in my name. This unusual spelling of my name causes common mispronunciations, as well as misspellings, even to this day. My grandfather always knew there was a "Y" in my name somewhere, but in spelling it, he was never able to put it in the same place; hence, his diverse spellings of my name as Carymn, Camryn, and Carmny.

The Danish poet, Soren Kierkegaard, wrote, "Life can only be understood backwards; but it must be lived forwards."

For most of my life that "Y" in my name was a reminder that I felt like a misplaced "why." Looking back, it was clear why Carmyn was my chosen name, especially the "Y" in my name. When I was three-years-old, a brilliant Ball of Light surrounded me whenever my perpetrators violated my will. I live now to bear witness to the Light. And that Light has become my friend for life. This was the beginning of several times in later years when the beautiful and resplendent Light appeared in my life; but it was years later before the Light revealed Himself and I would understand what happened back then.

Many were envious of my seemingly privileged life as a wealthy, society debutante, but underneath the ball gowns and jewels, there was a tormented love-starved little girl.

Do you recall the first time you became aware people were "looking" at you?

For me, I remember the exact location and time I became self-conscious others were watching me.

It was my first day of school in September, 1954.

As other students rode the bus, walked to school or were dropped off by a parent, I pulled up in the back seat of a large black Cadillac, driven by a chauffeur. As Willie D. led me into school that first day, not only did the kids look at me, but adults stared as well. I wanted to close my eyes and disappear.

The next day, I asked Willy D. to drop me off six blocks from school so I could walk like the other kids. It only made it worse because he followed behind me in that huge car. I looked like the emperor with no clothes, which only made everyone stare and laugh more.

That day marked the beginning of my feeling different, out of place, and misunderstood. I wanted to be anybody but me; if only I could change my name and be someone else. I felt different, unacceptable, and misunderstood.

These feelings, along with a traumatic and abusive childhood of incest, left me disappointed and without hope. My endless repeated violations of rape resulted in an abortion because of the incest at age thirteen. It was the push over the edge into nothingness that tempted me to take my life to silence the pain inside.

After two failed suicide attempts, I married right out of high school at age eighteen. Due to the abusive relationship, I felt trapped, and this marriage ended in divorce, nineteen months later.

Life was not working for me.

It seems I tried everything: money, marriage, and fame. I planned to achieve fame by becoming a model. At 5'10" I weighed 114 pounds so I could get into a size four. Three weeks before I was scheduled to leave for New York City to stake my claim to fame, I met a handsome blue-eyed wonder. When he stood up to introduce himself, he gently removed his black-rimmed glasses and put them in his coat pocket.

"Hi," this gorgeous man said as he stuck out his hand to shake mine.

Well, he might as well have said, "Hi, I am Clark Kent, and Superman is here to take you away, baby!" And I did go!

Expecting a husband and children to give me the unconditional love and acceptance my loved-starved heart longed to have, I was greatly disillusioned after two years of marriage.

One day, at age twenty-four, after I put my two daughters, two-years-old and six months old, down for their naps, I found my husband's 20-gauge shotgun, and decided to end it all. I would not fail this time. But how do you hold a shotgun up to your head? Suddenly, my six-month-old started crying, then she woke my two-year-old, and she was crying. I glanced up and saw my reflection in the mirror, holding that shotgun.

What am I doing? I started crying and pleading, "Whatever your name is in heaven, and if you really are, help!"

Three weeks later I was invited to a Christian Coffee Hour on December 17. I thought it was a mistake; it should be called a *Christmas* Coffee Hour. It was my sister-in-law's event, so I felt obligated to go.

The only times I had been exposed to church was when my alcoholic mother took me to the early morning Communion service. All they did was sit and stand, sit, stand and kneel. I finally got so tired I sat on the floor with my back against the pew. Over the altar was a huge cross with Jesus hanging on it. The minister quoted from the Book of Common Prayer, "God gave His only Begotten Son." I never knew what "begotten" was, but I thought he said, "forgotten." I felt sorry for Jesus, as I knew how he felt to be forgotten by His family as well.

The Christmas Coffee was uncomfortable for me, especially when a woman got up to give her testimony. She had been divorced. Me too. She had been depressed and wanted to die. Me too. She felt lost without any answers to life. Me too!

Then she did a weird thing; she prayed. I had only heard a priest lead others in prayer, never a woman. At the end of her prayer she said, "If anyone here has never received Christ, I am going to say a prayer to pray along with me."

That was one thing I had never done, so what the heck, might as well try that. I prayed, "Yeah I have sinned, sure know that" and then I asked Jesus into my heart.

The girl I came with bolted after it was over. When we got to the car she said, "I can't believe anybody would be so dumb to pray a prayer like that." I thought I was anything but dumb so I said, "Me, too."

Two months went by and on February 19, 1974, at 3 a.m., I was reading Hal Lindsey's *Late Great Planet Earth*. I was terrified about the end of the world and the judgment of God sounded horrific.

I wondered *where I would be if this happened?* Then in parenthesis, the book asked, (Have you ever received Christ? Where is He?). By the way, I never found that sentence in that book when I went back to it later. But at that moment, since I am a visual person, I remembered Christ on the cross and knew why Christ was there. He was there for me.

Christ died for me!

Then I imagined Jesus was right behind me. I stood up and turned around, only to fall to my knees.

I felt the warm love of Jesus Christ pour over my head, and I grabbed my chest and said, "You are here." It was the first time in my life I felt loved, accepted, and understood. I was forgiven, totally and completely forgiven of all my sins.

I had been bitter within, angry at God, and at life. I lived a life of great pretend on the outside, but with great pain on the inside.

Let's imagine to get into heaven, our requirement is to swim from California to Hawaii. In this competition are the following people: Mother Teresa, Mahatma Gandhi, Buddha, King David, The Pope, Billy Graham, most of us, Brad Pitt, and Oprah Winfrey. Then there is a liar, the adulterer, the thief, Charles Manson, Jack the Ripper, Hitler, and the pilots of the airplanes that hit the World Trade Center Towers.

Mother Teresa swims 500 miles; the Pope swims 800 miles; Billy Graham, 1,000; Gandhi, 300; you and I make it 75 miles; Jack the Ripper and Hitler immediately sink. The point is no one is going to make it; every single one is going to fall way short of the Hawaiian paradise! None of us are going to make it on our own; we all are going to fall short of a perfect and Holy God.

But that is not the end of the story. Just like God went to Cain and said, "Why are you angry?" God asks us and every other human being born on planet earth, "Why are you angry? If you do what is right, I have given you a way, the right way and the only way. The arms of my Son, Jesus Christ, are outstretched on the cross, dying for you to come to Him."

For you, Jesus Christ is the vessel to take you all the way to the warm beaches of God's love and acceptance. Jesus swam the shark-infested waters, went through the overwhelming waves of the treacherous storms of the dark sea and walked onto the warm beaches and sunlit lush paradise. He invites us to come.

And if there was only you in the ocean, Jesus would come for you alone.

God came to me and said, "Why are you angry? Why are you depressed? Why are you hopeless? If you choose life in my Son, will not your countenance be lifted?"

No matter where we are in life, no matter what we have done, God is seeking us; God comes to us; He eagerly responds to those who cry out to Him, just as I did.

The option was clear; the journey on either path that I was taking was determined by something as simple as a choice. February 19. 1974, was the divine moment in my life when I chose Jesus Christ.

My life has never been the same since. Yes, I still confront problems in my life. However, through understanding, God loves me right where I am; I can forgive and possibly never forget.

God provided my choice in His Son, and Jesus assures me, "Your past is truly your past. Now, I ask what do you want your future to be?"

I am thankful God rescued me from the deep waters that threatened to overtake me. God also has a life vest with your name on it. Will you reach out and grab it?

Carmyn and her husband, Hal, founded Breakthrough Ministries, LLC in 2013. Carmyn has taught on a regular basis in women's ministry in various churches in Fort Worth, Texas and Tulsa, Oklahoma since 1981. She is a speaker at women's organizations, church groups and retreats. Find Carmyn at carmynsparks.com.

Thoughts to Ponder
from Why Ask Why?

1. God knows the answers to all your "why" questions.

2. God gazes at you with love, not judgment.

3. God responds to those who cry out to Him.

> ### *What "why" questions do you want God to answer?*

She said, "Why is this happening to me?"
So she went to inquire of the Lord. — Genesis 25:22

Taming of a Wildcat
by Bill Billard

Are you a cat lover? As a small boy, I had a deep affection for cats. Early on, I learned how cats always land on their feet, and because of their incredible agility, cats have nine lives. I believed it! Back then, I could never imagine there was a possibility I could also have nine lives. I say that because I am about to celebrate the twelfth birthday of my seventh life.

I don't have a hidden furry tail, so I am probably not part cat, and no, I haven't died and come back to life six times. I have, however, had six close encounters with death. I courageously admit I chose three of those close encounters, and because of my bad choices, for many years I suffered from periods of deep depression and suicidal thought patterns.

Sensitivity to rejection, unresolved conflicts from years gone by, and a profound sense I was not good enough continuously flooded my thoughts. I lived a life filled with overwhelming feelings of rejection, humiliation, and a desperate, lonely desire to be accepted. I hated the intensity of all of those raw emotions confronting me daily. I thought the best way to deal with the pain was to find ways to distract attention away from it. That "head in the sand" strategy led me deep into marijuana use and casual sex as a cover up for my constant hopelessness.

On the outside, I did my best to be a skillful provider for my family, but my marijuana addiction and lack of clear focus kept me dissatisfied with even the most promising opportunities in the field of electronic technology. I trained to excel, but I walked away from many good jobs excusing the separation as a fault of the job; the boss, the company, or whatever "reason" I thought would explain away my disregard for a need to be clear-minded and solution-focused.

My despair and self-loathing reached a tormenting point toward the end of 1975, when I decided to end my life. In the moments surrounding my decision to die, I reflected on how my act would affect my family, and I decided to end it all by setting fire to my home. The fire would be considered an "accidental death" and my family would be spared the shame of suicide. After smoking several joints, I lit the match, started the fire, and then settled into a bathtub full of water to keep my body from being consumed by the flames.

I survived that dreadful decision, but then faced a charge of arson for setting the fire. In jail awaiting trial, hopelessness struck again, and I attempted to take my life again because I thought I would surely face many years in prison. However, to my amazement, I received a hopeful letter in the mail. After taking an overdose of medicine that I had squirreled away under my bunk, I was still lucid enough to read. The letter from my attorney said there was a probability of a reprieve from imprisonment. With that stirring of hope, I voluntarily sought help in recovering from my poor choice.

I decided I could use my skills and power to help myself recover and reassess the circumstances that led me down such a dark path, so for the next month, I sat all day journaling an account of the experiences that had overtaken me. It helped me temporarily and gave evidence to the judge handling my case, that probation for my choices was appropriate.

Yes, I avoided prison; but I also avoided accepting actual responsibility for the underlying issues of my poor decisions.

Shortly after my release, I was back to my sex, drugs, and rock and roll lifestyle. I remained in this depraved indifference to life for another ten years, stringing one bad decision after another. I roamed from Florida to California and many places in between.

I sought to put together a "stable" life on the outside, but relied solely on the self-medication, via drugs and sex, as the foundation of my deepest motivation and desires. I clearly stated to my second wife, Marcia, "I don't know what I want to be when I grow up. Meanwhile, I want to have fun and play hard while I still can."

Have there been times in your life where you have found ways to escape from the painful memories of your past?

At age 40, "playtime" came to a jolting halt in the mountain valleys of Northern California. I made a meager living as a professional gold miner. In my "strike it rich" gambling mentality, I spent three years gold dredge mining on the Klamath River and finding the minute amounts of gold that kept me in food, pot and gas for the next day's possibility of the jackpot treasure.

For more than six months I ignored the growing painful lump in my right bicep. Finally, the pain and the lump grew too big and too painful to ignore.

My doctor delivered the worst-case scenario. "You have cancer; we have scheduled you for surgery to amputate your arm at the shoulder." I am sorry to say the surgery will give you relief from the pain and slow the spread of your cancer, but it will not be a cure. We may be able to slow the process, but you probably will not survive for more than six months."

The shock of that news was devastating; however, it was the beginning of the sobering journey I needed to take as I began my fourth life journey. That journey commenced with time alone and the wise choice to take a day to collect my thoughts.

I climbed high up on the mountainside, and in that quiet setting began to think carefully about what was paramount and about whether there was any real value in what my life had accomplished. I thought about what I allowed myself to believe, justifying my choice to isolate myself in that river valley, totally disconnected from my family and consumed by the relevant meaninglessness of my mining "quest." I was neither rich, nor had I created any legacy to pass on. Now I was going to die.

I was raised to believe in God and to recognize the existence of life after death, but did I really believe it? Now I was not far away from some type of eternal future, if it was true. Did God actually exist? If so, was I going to spend eternity in Hell? While I was raised in a home that believed in God, I concluded God was a myth created in the past ages to induce fear and keep the masses under control. That conclusion made sense to my wander lusting, isolated and rejected heart. It sounded plausible and relevant to my rebellious spirit. But now in this compellingly quiet moment, I am asking, "Is my basic argument the truth?"

In the moments after asking that question, humbling doubt found its ground. Was my argument truer than what wiser men than me discovered? The men that tested the truth of their conclusions for most of recorded history? Finally, how could I be so arrogant to believe I had the truth about the motives of the men who honored God as a real being, and not just a myth or legend?

On that mountainside in those deeply reflective moments, a change began to grow within in me. It was not a sudden return to God and a life of faith, but it was enough for me to catch a glimmer of what life could be for me. I walked home with a changed perspective. I somehow knew I was going to live in spite of my cancer, but I had no idea what turn my life was beginning to take. I just knew that life was a precious gift and in that simple truth there is hope.

Over the next several weeks my medical outlook changed dramatically. The origin of my cancer was re-diagnosed and determined to be far less life threatening. There was no spread of the tumor, and surgery was performed to remove it from my arm.

If my life were a fairy tale, I would immediately learn how to be cat-like and land on my feet. Afterward, life would be easy and perfectly beautiful.

In real life, progress is much slower when you are untangling the effects of years of depraved thinking. Within three months, I made a decision to separate myself from all of the disruptive habits I engaged in for seventeen years.

Without looking back, I left drugs, casual sex, and the gambling mentality of "strike it rich" gold mining and moved back to my family home in Texas. I returned home to a warm welcome, and I began to build real relationships with others.

The most significant of those new relationships started my first day home. My sister and her husband, Dennis, also returned to Texas that day. Dennis had just retired from twenty years of naval service, and they too had decided to make Texas their home as well. We became fast friends, and his friendship showed me the value of honesty, compassion, and consideration. Without effort, he became my mentor.

The tragedy of a cancer diagnosis struck again in my life, but this time, I was not the victim. It was Dennis. For the next seven years, Dennis lived a heroic life of submitting to chemotherapy, followed by periods of remission, followed by the next advance of his disease. Then finally, Dennis said his last good-byes at home and passed away quietly, surrounded by his family.

Before Dennis, I never had a real true friend relationship with another man. There were superficial acquaintances, but never the valued, open honesty that characterizes true love and honor. I was not prepared to meet life without my best friend. I did not have any idea that I would deeply grieve the end of our friendship, and I was not ready to know how to deal with the dark void of love confronting me. My relationship with my wife Marcia was about the convenience of companionship and codependency, not a sincere, loving commitment.

I longed to have real meaning and honest love as the foundation of my life. Marcia and I agreed that our life together should come to a close. For the first time in my life, I took the time to think carefully about what mattered to me. I started by determining how I would find a genuine and loving relationship.

The next year was a slow process of inner domestication from alley cat to house cat. I spent time carefully considering what I valued most in both my environment and in my relationships. I could more clearly define a healthy living environment. But deep inside, I yearned for a relationship based on acceptance of my strengths, as well as my weaknesses. More than anything, I longed to be considered worthy of honest enduring love.

I met Laura through Match.com. We chatted via email and then finally by phone before agreeing to have our first date. In our first face-to-face meeting, I fell in love with the nurturing grandmother who made no excuses as she busily tended to the care of her nine-month-old grandson Ben.

During moments of quiet conversation, later in the evening, Laura asked me specifically about my faith in God. My best answer was that I did believe in God as the creator of all things and that I honored him for the beauty of His creation. It was not the answer Laura wanted to hear, but she accepted me into her life as a work in progress.

I cautiously accepted her invitation to join her in regular attendance at church. Knowing I had my relationship with her at stake, I walked into a church for the first time in thirty-two years. My anxiety about possibly being rejected by

God and the people of God evaporated in my first experience. Instead of meeting a group of stern-faced rule keepers, I met a group of open, caring, loving new friends who accepted me and who openly loved God in their joyous praise of him. In that one experience, I knew without a doubt, God was real, and that I could learn to love Him as well.

Within a year, Laura and I married. It was a drama filled relationship because we spent much of our time caring for and nurturing her son Barry, whose health rapidly deteriorated from an incurable disease. Yes, you probably guessed right, Barry had cancer. He passed away six months after our vows, and I wanted to be the rock of support Laura deserved to have as a husband; but as a new believer, I still wasn't as strong as I should have been during that trial.

However, my awareness of God's presence grew immensely over the next twelve years. There for me through the most difficult moments, I learned how much I could trust Him as he healed me completely from an accident that crushed a vertebra in my spine. In that learning, my outlook transformed from despair at the probability of my future as a cripple not capable of continuing my difficult life as a handyman, to a conviction that God was right there beside me, and I could trust Him completely for a full recovery. He fulfilled my hope beyond my wildest imagination. He erased all of my pain, and I returned to a normal routine in just a few days.

Just one short year later, I suffered a second catastrophic accident. This one left me in complete paralysis. I learned how intimate and tender deep prayerful moments with God could be as He nurtured and taught me. While I learned from the Great Teacher, He restored my health. God transformed me once again from being completely incapacitated to full restoration. Yes, the accident broke my body, but not my hopeful, trusting spirit.

I made it all the way through both of those experiences in complete peace and quiet calm. They changed the person I am in the most dramatic ways possible. I now experience each moment in unshakable confidence that I do not walk alone. He is always with me.

I struggle moment-to-moment to describe adequately how intensely God poured out his love to us. John 3:16 says, "God loves every one of us so much He gave up His only Son, a part of himself, so that whoever could believe that he is a real person, would have the opportunity to spend all eternity sharing life with Him."

Can you remember the most intense experience you ever had being loved by another person? Was that tender moment more precious and beautiful than you can describe? If you could, would you distill the beauty of the moment and put it in a spray bottle to carry with you? You could pull it out, spritz yourself and experience that same intensity all over again whenever you wanted.

Would you have your bottle with you all the time?

Would you ever lose that bottle?

If someone could discover how to pour God's love into a bottle like that, it would sell in the most exclusive shops, and the wealthiest of men would be willing to pay more than the entire lifetime earnings of the average person for it. They would be standing in line for their bottle because they would have heard that. Just one tiny drop of it would instantly reward them with the greatest intensity of love they ever experienced. It would be perfect, fulfilling, overwhelmingly tender, and compelling beyond all of the experiences of love in their entire life combined, and it would change their life forever.

Fortunately for each of us, God is not a merchant selling His love to the highest bidder. He gives it all away for free! Father God continually pours it out into each and every one of our lives in an endless stream of love through the unstoppable power of His Spirit presence. In fact, He is recording every precious moment of our life here on this earth. When we spend the rest of eternity with Him, we will have the precious gift of memories restored to us. Even better, we will be able to experience those memories anytime we want; not in the small sometimes insignificant way they are perceived now, but from the grandest perspective possible through His eyes.

To God, every moment is precious, sacred and intensely valued. If you could, wouldn't you sincerely desire to experience your life in that kind of way? Wouldn't that be precious to you beyond your wildest imagination?

I have made several references to my cat-like nature as I share my story with you. No, I do not think I am a part cat and part man. I am truly grateful to be one of God's human creations. I know that every moment of my life, He has been patiently tending to the creation process within me. He lovingly informs every cell with all the information it needs to have a healthy life, and he gives me wise, clear insight by the commanding presence of His Spirit living in me. He shows me what the next best choice is for me to make in my life and my relationships.

I could, if I choose, believe that I am a cat person living a "charmed life" and ignore the still small voice within me. However, I chose that ignorant path for far too many years, and I do not want to live a life of despair now that I have opted for a life of peace and joy and personal agreement with Him. More than anything, I would not want to give up sharing my life in eternity with the Lord, my dearest best friend.

I've learned the life I now live is the life that promises an eternal future. Even if it ended today, my next life would be in Heaven. I am grateful for God's intervention. Like a cat, I've finally landed on my feet!

Bill Billard is a Texas transplant from New York City. He and his wife, Laura, have four daughters and eight grandchildren. Bill is the author of The Healing Power of God's Love My Journey which will be published in November 2016. His passion is lay-led ministry.

Thoughts to Ponder
from Taming of a Wildcat

1. God has enough love to fill any empty heart.

2. Search for Him instead of substitutes.

3. Every day is a precious gift from God.

**How are you a good steward
of the one life you have been given?**

The law from your mouth is more precious to me than thousands of pieces of silver and gold. — Psalm 119:72

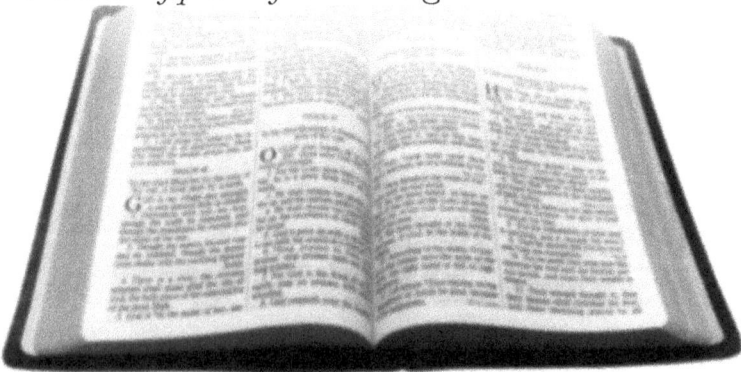

God's Good News for You

Now that you have read these stories of great faith, you may want to know how you can have this same kind of faith. We have Good News for you!

He loves you!

For this is the way God loved the world: He gave his one and only Son, so that everyone who believes in him will not perish but have eternal life. — John 3:16 (NET)

He wants to meet your need.

It's your sins that have cut you off from God. Because of your sins, he has turned away and will not listen anymore. — Isaiah 59:2 (NLT)

For God made Christ, who never sinned, to be the offering for our sin, so that we could be made right with God through Christ. — 2 Corinthians 5:21 (NLT)

He offers you a free gift!

For the payoff of sin is death, but the gift of God is eternal life in Christ Jesus our Lord. — Romans 6:23 (NET)

How to receive this gift:

If you openly declare that Jesus is Lord and believe in your heart that God raised him from the dead, you will be saved. For it is by believing in your heart that you are made right with God, and it is by openly declaring your faith that you are saved. — Romans 10:9 (NLT)

Jesus, I recognize I have sinned and need You. I believe You are the Son of God, that You died on the cross for my sin, rose from the dead and now sit at the right hand of God. I trust You alone and choose to follow You. Thank you for forgiving me of my sin and giving me eternal life. In Jesus' name, Amen.

If you have chosen to receive God's gift or would like more information, please contact us at info@RoaringLambs.org. We would love to hear from you!

Share With Us

Roaring Lambs is working on our next volume of *Stories of Roaring Faith*, a book of testimonies designed to lead a nonbeliever to faith in Jesus Christ, and to encourage the followers of Jesus. We would love to consider your testimony. To have your testimony reviewed, please send us via email or mail your typed, double-spaced, approximately 3,000-word story.

Email: info@RoaringLambs.org
Address: 17110 Dallas Parkway, Suite 220
            Dallas, TX 75248

We ask that you submit it no later than July 1st for consideration in the next volume. If chosen, you will receive a Release Form giving us permission to edit and include your testimony.

In addition, you will be considered as a guest on our radio show, *A Time to Dream*, which also features life-changing testimonies.

Let God use your story by writing, submitting, and sharing what He has done for you.

Roaring Lambs Ministries is a 501(c)(3), which exists on tax deductible donations.

We would welcome any gifts to sustain our ministry to equip believers to better communicate their faith. Donations may be mailed to the address above or be made online at www.RoaringLambs.org.

There are many ways to give to Roaring Lambs: check, credit card, gifts of stock or real estate, planned gifts by will or trust. Roaring Lambs can help with any of the above by working with your attorney or accountant.

"Give, and it will be given to you. A good measure, pressed down, shaken together and running over, will be poured into your lap. For with the measure you use, it will be measured to you." — Luke 6:38

About the Editors

With a heart for God, people, and business, Donna stays active in the Christian community. She has been involved with this ministry since its inception and came on staff in 2008. Donna oversees all Roaring Lambs events and Bible studies, and she co-hosts an international radio show called, *A Time to Dream* on the WRNO Worldwide Radio Network. The program features powerful faith stories. She especially enjoys speaking to ladies groups, churches, and retreats. Her rich Jewish heritage and her study of God's Word enhance her insight into the issues involved in Christian faith and living. In addition to her work with Roaring Lambs, Donna serves on the Fellowship of Professional Women Board, the Christian Women in Media Advisory Committee, and the Collin County Christian Prayer Breakfast Committee.

Answering God's call at the age of nine to become a "missionary," Belinda's mission was to touch others with the Good News of Jesus Christ. Her passion has been equipping believers to effectively live life with hope, purpose, and strength. She has done this as a pastor's daughter, pastor's wife, administrator, Bible study teacher, speaker, and writer. She has served in many churches and ministries, including Hope for the Heart, Marketplace Ministries, and Roaring Lambs.

Belinda's great joy is her husband, four daughters and fourteen grandchildren. She currently resides in Carrollton, Texas and is employed with Roaring Lambs Ministries. She can be contacted at bmcbride@roaringlambs.org

Lisa Burkhardt Worley is an award winning author and speaker, and is the Director of Special Projects for Roaring Lambs Ministries. She is also the founder of Pearls of Promise Ministries. Lisa has co-authored three books, the *Pearls of Promise* devotional, *If I Only Had*, and *The Most Powerful P: A Child's Introduction to the Power of Prayer*. She is a former national and local television sportscaster, and after a sixteen-year hiatus, she is now back in the media, co-hosting an international weekly radio show with Donna Skell called *A Time to Dream* on the WRNO-Worldwide Radio Network. Lisa earned a Master's of Theological Studies degree from Perkins School of Theology

For ten years, Frank Ball directed North Texas Christian Writers to help members improve their writing skills. He founded Story Help Groups (www.StoryHelpGroups.org) in 2011 to encourage and equip all Christians to tell their life-changing stories. Besides his speaking engagements and writing his own books, he does ghostwriting, copy editing, and graphic design to help others publish high-quality books. As Pastor of Biblical Research and Writing for three years, he wrote sermons, teaching materials, and hundreds of devotions. He coaches writers and writes blogs. He's a panelist on The Writers' View. His book *Eyewitness: The Life of Christ Told in One Story* is a compilation of biblical information on the life of Christ in a chronological story that reads like a novel. His website is www.FrankBall.org.